3/02

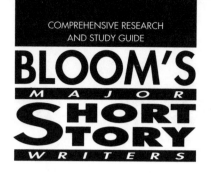

COMPREHENSIVE RESEARCH
AND STUDY GUIDE

BLOOM'S
MAJOR
SHORT
STORY
WRITERS

Joseph

Conrad

EDITED AND WITH AN
INTRODUCTION BY HAROLD BLOOM

CURRENTLY AVAILABLE

BLOOM'S MAJOR SHORT STORY WRITERS

Anton Chekhov

Joseph Conrad

Stephen Crane

William Faulkner

F. Scott Fitzgerald

Nathaniel Hawthorne

Ernest Hemingway

O. Henry

Shirley Jackson

Henry James

James Joyce

D. H. Lawrence

Jack London

Herman Melville

Flannery O'Connor

Edgar Allan Poe

Katherine Anne Porter

J. D. Salinger

John Steinbeck

Mark Twain

John Updike

Eudora Welty

BLOOM'S MAJOR WORLD POETS

Maya Angelou

Robert Browning

Geoffrey Chaucer

Samuel T. Coleridge

Dante

Emily Dickinson

John Donne

T. S. Eliot

Robert Frost

Homer

Langston Hughes

John Keats

John Milton

Sylvia Plath

Edgar Allan Poe

Poets of World War I

Shakespeare's Poems & Sonnets

Percy Shelley

Alfred, Lord Tennyson

Walt Whitman

William Wordsworth

William Butler Yeats

COMPREHENSIVE RESEARCH
AND STUDY GUIDE

BLOOM'S
MAJOR
SHORT STORY
WRITERS

Joseph
Conrad

EDITED AND W   BLOOM

© 2001 by Chelsea House Publishers, a subsidiary of
Haights Cross Communications.

Introduction © 2001 by Harold Bloom.

Printed and bound in the United States of America.

First Printing
1 3 5 7 9 8 6 4 2

Library of Congress Cataloging-in-Publication Data
Joseph Conrad / Harold Bloom, ed.
     p. cm. — (Bloom's major short story writers)
  Includes bibliographical references and index.
  ISBN 0-7910-5940-5
   1. Conrad, Joseph, 1857–1924—Criticism and interpretation—
Handbooks, manuals, etc. 2. Conrad, Joseph, 1857–1924—
Examinations—Study guides. 3. Short story—Examinations—
Study guides. 4. Short story Handbooks, manuals, etc.
I. Bloom, Harold. II. Series.

PR6005.O4 Z7499 2000
823'.912—dc21   00-024062
                                      CIP

Chelsea House Publishers
1974 Sproul Road, Suite 400
Broomall, PA 19008-0914

The Chelsea House World Wide Web address is
http://www.chelseahouse.com

Contributing Editor: Pamela Loos

Produced by: Robert Gerson Publisher's Services, Avondale, PA

Contents

User's Guide

This volume is designed to present biographical, critical, and biblio-graphical information on the author's best-known or most important short stories. Following Harold Bloom's editor's note and introduction is a detailed biography of the author, discussing major life events and important literary accomplishments. A plot summary of each short story follows, tracing significant themes, patterns, and motifs in the work, and an annotated list of characters supplies brief information on the main characters in each story.

A selection of critical extracts, derived from previously published mate-rial from leading critics, analyzes aspects of each short story. The extracts consist of statements from the author, if available, early reviews of the work, and later evaluations up to the present. A bibliography of the author's writings (including a complete list of all books written, cowritten, edited, and translated), a list of additional books and articles on the author and the work, and an index of themes and ideas in the author's writings conclude the volume.

∾

Harold Bloom is Sterling Professor of the Humanities at Yale University and Henry W. and Albert A. Berg Professor of English at the New York University Graduate School. He is the author of over 20 books, including *Shelley's Mythmaking* (1959), *The Visionary Company* (1961), *Blake's Apocalypse* (1963), *Yeats* (1970), *A Map of Misreading* (1975), *Kabbalah and Criticism* (1975), *Agon: Toward a Theory of Revisionism* (1982), *The American Religion* (1992), *The Western Canon* (1994), and *Omens of Millennium: The Gnosis of Angels, Dreams, and Resurrection* (1996). *The Anxiety of Influence* (1973) sets forth Professor Bloom's provocative theory of the literary relationships between the great writers and their predecessors. His most recent books include *Shake-speare: The Invention of the Human,* a 1998 National Book Award finalist, and *How to Read and Why,* which was published in 2000.

Professor Bloom earned his Ph.D. from Yale University in 1955 and has served on the Yale faculty since then. He is a 1985 MacArthur Founda-tion Award recipient, served as the Charles Eliot Norton Professor of Poetry at Harvard University in 1987–88, and has received honorary degrees from the universities of Rome and Bologna. In 1999, Professor Bloom received the prestigious American Academy of Arts and Letters Gold Medal for Criticism.

Currently, Harold Bloom is the editor of numerous Chelsea House volumes of literary criticism, including the series BLOOM'S NOTES, BLOOM'S MAJOR DRAMATISTS, BLOOM'S MAJOR NOVELISTS, MAJOR LITERARY CHARACTERS, MODERN CRITICAL VIEWS, MODERN CRITICAL INTERPRETATIONS, and WOMEN WRITERS OF ENGLISH AND THEIR WORKS.

Editor's Note

My Introduction argues a critical preference for "Typhoon" and *The Shadow-Line* over the better-known "Heart of Darkness" and "The Secret Sharer."

As there are more than thirty critical extracts, I commend particularly Lionel Trilling and Chinua Achebe on "Heart of Darkness," though their views diverge sharply.

Edward W. Said and H. M. Daleskie show particular insight into "The Secret Sharer," while F. R. Leavis and Ian Watt, both exemplary critics of prose fiction, illuminate *The Shadow-Line* from perspectives that reinforce one another.

Frederick R. Karl cogently asserts the strength in the final pages of "Typhoon."

Introduction

HAROLD BLOOM

The full greatness of Joseph Conrad is manifested in the sequence of his major novels: *Nostromo* (1904), *The Secret Agent* (1907), *Under Western Eyes* (1911), and *Victory* (1915). Yet the four tales or longer stories examined in this volume have achieved permanent popularity, and at the least are an appropriate introduction to Conrad. The most famous, "Heart of Darkness," seems to me the most flawed, primarily because neither Conrad nor his narrator, Marlow, is at all clear as to just what Kurtz means, or ought to mean. And yet "Heart of Darkness" has been a central influence upon the American imagination: its legatees include Eliot's *The Waste Land*, Scott Fitzgerald's *The Great Gatsby*, Hemingway's *The Sun Also Rises*, Faulkner's *Absalom, Absalom!*, and the movies of Welles and Coppola. It may be that the tale's essential obscurantism has helped to make it inescapable as a crucial twentieth-century parable of the Fall of Man.

Henry James, Conrad's friendly rival, protested Marlow's role as "mystic mariner," who quests to the interior or heart of darkness without apparent purpose. Conrad however felt very comfortable with Marlow, perhaps too much so. Any reader may ask: is Marlow at all changed by his quest for Kurtz?

Does Marlow (or Conrad) condescend to Africa and the Africans? The distinguished Nigerian novelist Chinua Achebe urges that judgment. If Achebe is too decisive in his view, it would only be that Conrad's obscurantism makes it too hard to tell just what this cautionary tale is about.

"Typhoon," in contrast, seems clarity itself, since Captain MacWhirr has every virtue except imagination. And yet MacWhirr has the sense, skill, and courage to sail straight through the typhoon, saving both ship and crew. After displaying devotion and astonishing competence, MacWhirr is principally memorable for saying of his steam ship: "I shouldn't like to lose her." Conrad wonderfully responds: "He was spared that annoyance," and we see that the apparently ordinary MacWhirr is the anti-Kurtz, and perhaps the anti-Marlow also.

"The Secret Sharer" is perhaps too much invested in clarity, and in surely too overt a symbolism. The Captain gives his hat to Leggatt, his secret sharer or other self, and the hat floats back to save the captain and vessel. And yet we care about the Captain and his story, since all of us have undergone the ordeal of beginnings, and "The Secret Sharer" is a central parable of the cost of confirmation that any initiation requires.

Of these four tales, I myself like *The Shadow-Line* best, perhaps because like *Victory* it is the work of Conrad entering the twilight, and studying the nostalgias with an elegiac grace. Conrad himself warned against any supernatural interpretation of *The Shadow-Line,* but there is a touch of Coleridge's *Rime of the Ancient Mariner* about the tale. We confront, with the novice Captain, a series of calamities so unrelenting that the ship indeed seems under a spell. And yet these disasters adequately represent all the bad luck, mistakes, and sorrows of conscience that many (if not all) of us must confront and stand up against. The reader, like the young Captain, comes through, with at least the possibility of an enhanced sense of self. ❀

Biography of
Joseph Conrad

"It seems impossible for him to make an ugly or insignificant movement of the pen." So wrote Virginia Woolf about Joseph Conrad in her book *The Common Reader*. "One opens his pages and feels as Helen must have felt when she looked in her glass and realised that, do what she would, she could never in any circumstances pass for a plain woman." Indeed, just as Conrad would not write plain words, neither would he live a plain life.

He was born Józef Teodor Konrad Nalecz Korzeniowski in Berdiczew, a town in Russian-occupied Poland, on December 3, 1857. As early as 1862, his father, Apollo Nalecz, was taken into penal exile in Siberia for helping to organize the secret Polish National Committee; Conrad and his mother, Eva, went with him. All three became sick, and Eva died of tuberculosis, devastating the seven-year-old boy. Conrad then spent much time taking care of his father, who also had contracted tuberculosis, although the child himself was frail, nervous, and often ill. Taught at home by his father, who wanted the boy to learn nothing of the Russians they hated, Conrad would escape loneliness by reading avidly. He had a strong literary education, since his father was a poet, playwright, and translator. Yet by May of 1869, Conrad's father had died and the boy was taken into the care of his uncle.

By October of 1874, Conrad convinced his uncle to let him enter the French merchant marine, and he made three voyages to the West Indies. In March of 1878, he shot himself in the chest after ending an unhappy love affair, although he told others the injury was the result of a duel. He was saved from the bullet, and also from debt, by his uncle, and then set out to sea with the English merchant navy.

Over the next sixteen years, Conrad landed in such exotic places as Australia, South America, India, Borneo, and the South Pacific. By 1886, he became master of his own ship; he also became a British subject and changed his name to Joseph Conrad. He became seriously ill with malaria after taking a job in the Congo with a Belgian company, retired from the sea in 1894, and settled in England.

Conrad had written his first story, "The Black Mate," in 1886 for a competition in a magazine, but wrote nothing more until 1889, when he started *Almayer's Folly*. When it was completed after three years, all reviews were encouraging, some coming from such distinguished writers as Henry James and H. G. Wells, and Conrad became friendly with many leading writers. He published *An Outcast of the Islands* in 1896 and the same year married Jessie George, with whom he would later have two sons. During the next two years, he published *The Nigger of the "Narcissus"* and *Tales of Unrest*. In 1899 Conrad's "Heart of Darkness" was published in three installments in *Blackwood's Edinburgh Magazine*. By 1900 he published *Lord Jim* and by 1902 *Typhoon and Youth*, a collection of short stories.

A shift now occurred in the subject of Conrad's work. While he previously had drawn on his experiences at sea, now he explored politics, first producing *Nostromo* in 1904, then *The Secret Agent* in 1907, and *Under Western Eyes* in 1911. Still, Conrad and his wife lived an uneasy life. They were plagued with money and health problems. Conrad would negotiate advances for writing, which would affect his nerves and bring on fevers and gout symptoms. A biographer, Frederick R. Karl, wrote of Conrad: "Apparently, he could not work effectively unless he were close to breakdown, on the edge of psychic disorders, ill in body and mind. Conrad's physical disorders were legion. . . . These, however, were simply the tip. The inner disorder was far greater, and when it was at its most intense, he functioned most effectively artistically." By 1910, Conrad suffered a nervous breakdown, yet he persisted with his writing.

Autobiographical reminiscences were published in *The Mirror of the Sea* in 1906 and *A Personal Record* in 1912. Semiautobiographical sea tales appeared as "The Secret Sharer," which was first published in installments in *Harper's Monthly Magazine* in 1910, and in the collection *'Twixt Land and Sea* (1912). By 1913 Conrad achieved mainstream popularity with *Chance*, which was launched with a strong advertising campaign in America by Alfred Knopf of Doubleday Publishers. This was the beginning of financial security and fame. Closely following were *Victory* (1915), *The Shadow-Line* (1917), *The Arrow of Gold* (1919), and *The Rescue* (1920). In 1923, Conrad visited America to give readings and arrived to much enthusiasm in New York Harbor. His last novel was *The Rover* (1923), which was followed by *Last Essays*, a nonfiction collection published posthumously. Conrad died on August 3, 1924, and was buried in Canterbury, England. ❀

Plot Summary of
"Heart of Darkness"

"Weaning those ignorant millions from their horrid ways" is heartily espoused near the opening of the "Heart of Darkness." This particular phrase comes from a representative English lady of the time, speaking about black Africans. As the tale persists, similar blatantly prejudiced, imperialistic views are voiced and acted upon by others, culminating in the ultimate, ironically savage call: "Exterminate all the brutes!"

Conrad ardently condemns such evil in this work, and stood as a bold radical as a result, for when it first was published Britain was in a fervor of colonization. By 1897 the British Empire ruled over a quarter of the world's population. While Conrad believed Britain's imperialistic methods were the least exploitative of native peoples, he abhorred those of the Russians, Germans, and Belgians. Aside from this insistence in "Heart of Darkness," Conrad also comments here on a range of issues, such as politics, civilization, psychology, morality, evolution, and man's understanding of himself. While at times his views seem clear, often they remain ambiguous, with the text shifting between realism, symbolism, and dream-like states.

"Heart of Darkness" is told through a narrator, who in turn allows Marlow to tell his story. Marlow, an experienced seaman, is on the deck of the yawl *Nellie,* which is sitting in the Thames River waiting for a shift in the tide. He has three listeners aside from the narrator. To them and us he tells his tale that starts with his aunt getting him a job as a captain on a steamship for a company of ivory traders. He learns that the position is open because his predecessor was killed during a fight with a village chief; an overwhelming ominousness pervades the story, not only from this but from numerous other incidents that occur that the reader uncovers.

Marlow leaves Europe and eventually lands at the company's lower station, which is worn, wasted, and chaotic. At the office Marlow meets the company's chief accountant, who is dressed impeccably and even has a starched collar. From him Marlow first hears of Kurtz, "a very remarkable person," who is the most successful of all the ivory-gathering agents. The accountant predicts he will "be somebody in the Administration before long."

Marlow then sets off on a 200-mile walk to the company's central station, after being delayed for ten hot days at the lower station. After fifteen days of strenuous traveling, he reaches the central station and finds that his steamboat is a wreck stuck at the bottom of the river. He immediately is told to meet with the manager, who Marlow initially believes to be very commonplace. The manager tells him that he and a few others had gotten in the steamboat in a rush to get up river because Kurtz's station was in "very grave, very grave" trouble. They are not sure if men there are dead, and he reiterates that Kurtz is very important to the company. Unfortunately, the boat had plowed into stones that had torn away her bottom before she had gotten very far. The manager tells Marlow he must set to work repairing his ship, anticipating it will take three months, which, it turns out, is exactly right.

Not long after Marlow has arrived, the men are drawn together when a shed of cheap trade goods catches on fire. It is here that Marlow meets a young agent, a man who the other agents keep away from because they believe he is the manager's spy. The young agent brings Marlow to his room, which has amenities that the others don't have, as well as collections of weapons.

The agent calls Kurtz a "prodigy . . . an emissary of pity and science and progress, and devil knows what else." He calls Kurtz part of the "new gang—the gang of virtue," the group of powerful people who had recommended Marlow for his job. These people believe in "higher intelligence, wide sympathies, a singleness of purpose," he explains. Marlow is surprised that the man believes he also has such powerful connections; it is the first time that a link between himself and Kurtz is made. The agent, whom Marlow calls a "papier mâché Mephistopheles," reveals that he wants to become the assistant to the present manager, and Marlow realizes that Kurtz's power upsets this agent and the manager.

Marlow returns to his boat; to him, work is an escape from the rest of this unreal place. "I like," he says, "what is in the work—the chance to find yourself." He also has become friendly with the mechanics, men of action who do good work.

The Eldorado Expedition arrives, its leader being the manager's uncle. Marlow overhears the two men talking and learns that the manager has provided Kurtz's inner station with no provisions for more than a year. They have heard no news from Kurtz for nine months, although they know that some months ago he made it 300 miles down the river with his shipment of ivory. He turned back though, and let his clerk continue the trip with the ivory, whereupon the manager heard how ill Kurtz was. Marlow relates how the two men get more frustrated as they talk of a man in Kurtz's district. "'Certainly,' grunted the other; 'get him hanged! Why not? Anything—anything can be done in this country.'"

After many more weeks, Marlow starts up river with the vile manager, three or four white men, and a crew of natives that will take care of the ship's engine. The trip seems interminable. In the heat of the unknown jungle, Marlow comments: ". . . there would be . . . a burst of yells, a whirl of black limbs, a mass of hands clapping, of feet stamping. . . . They howled and leaped, and spun, and made horrid faces; but what thrilled you was just the thought of their humanity—like yours—the thought of your remote kinship."

Suddenly, only a mile-and-a-half from the inner station the ship is bombarded with arrows. A spear kills the black helmsman that Marlow has befriended. Luckily, when Marlow blows the steamer's whistle, the men on shore stop the attack. The inner station appears, and a Russian man in patched, harlequin-like attire greets them from shore. He is Kurtz's devotee and student, and while Marlow talks with him the manager takes some men to go and get Kurtz. The Russian raves over the depth and range of subjects Kurtz has covered in his remarkable monologues. Even love is spoken of, and poetry, Kurtz's own included, is recited.

The harlequin explains that while they have had no trading supplies, Kurtz has still amassed a large collection of ivory by force. The natives see him as a god; he participates in their secret rites, has lost all control. Kurtz has been very ill, he says, and at times has even threatened to shoot the Russian, who has doctored him through bouts of severe illness.

Marlow looks in his spy-glass at the fence around the station and realizes that the round pieces atop the posts are not wood but actually dead men's heads. "They only showed that Mr. Kurtz lacked restraint in the gratification of his various lusts. . . . But the wilderness had found him out early, and had taken on him a terrible vengeance for the fantastic invasion. I think it had whispered to him things about himself which he did not know. . . . It echoed loudly within him because he was hollow at the core. . . ."

While Kurtz is very sick, the men manage to carry him aboard, although the natives on shore and a magnificent black mistress do not want him to go. At night Marlow realizes Kurtz has sneaked off the boat and decides not to tell anyone but to get him back at his own risk. Pitifully, Kurtz says when Marlow finds him, "I had immense plans." But Marlow realizes he is mad and readily is able to help him back to the ship. The next morning Kurtz is given a roaring farewell by the natives on shore.

Kurtz gives Marlow a collection of his private papers. A few days later, he dies, uttering a final cry, "The horror! The horror!"

Once again at the main station, Marlow has become ill and is sent back home. He brings Kurtz's pack of letters to the woman Kurtz was engaged to. She, like all the others who have spoken of the man, believes him amazing. When she presses Marlow about Kurtz's last words, he lies and tells her his last word was her name. With this, she feels she can heal. ❈

List of Characters in
"Heart of Darkness"

Charlie Marlow is the protagonist and dominant narrator. He is moral, sensitive, and described as sitting in a Buddha-like position as he relates his story. He is an experienced seaman who speaks of his first trip on fresh water.

Kurtz is the amazing charismatic manager of the inner station. He is the most successful ivory-gathering agent of the trading company and spoken of throughout the story as a larger-than-life man—a poet, philosopher, and musician—with "immense plans." We look forward to meeting him, just as Marlow does, only to find him a thief and murderer, enfeebled and quite mad. By his last breath we are led to believe that he has a "supreme moment," where he finally sees his complete self.

The *manager* of the ivory-trading company is "commonplace in complexion . . . of ordinary build" and has eyes that are "perhaps remarkably cold." While Marlow initially believes him a "chattering idiot," as the story progresses we find he is much more dangerous than that. He is a thorough villain. ✿

Critical Views on
"Heart of Darkness"

JOSEPH CONRAD ON MARLOW'S PURPOSE

[Between 1917 and 1920 Joseph Conrad wrote prefaces to his major works for the uniform edition of his *Collected Works* (published 1923–1938). In this extract from his introduction to *Youth,* Conrad describes what Marlow is supposed to be.]

'Youth' was not my first contribution to *Maga* ⟨*Blackwood's Edinburgh Magazine*⟩. It was the second. But that story marks the first appearance in the world of the man Marlow, with whom my relations have grown very intimate in the course of years. The origins of that gentleman (nobody as far as I know had ever hinted that he was anything but that)—his origins have been the subject of some literary speculation of, I am glad to say, a friendly nature.

One would think that I am the proper person to throw a light on the matter; but in truth I find that it isn't so easy. It is pleasant to remember that nobody had charged him with fraudulent purposes or looked down on him as a charlatan; but apart from that he was supposed to be all sorts of things; a clever screen, a mere device, a 'personator,' a familiar spirit, a whispering 'daemon.' I myself have been suspected of a meditated plan for his capture.

That is not so. I made no plans. The man Marlow and I came together in the casual manner of those health-resort acquaintances which sometimes ripen into friendships. This one has ripened. For all his assertiveness in matters of opinion he is not an intrusive person. He haunts my hours of solitude, when, in silence, we lay our heads together in great comfort and harmony; but as we part at the end of a tale I am never sure that it may not be for the last time. Yet I don't think that either of us would care much to survive the other. In his case, at any rate, his occupation would be gone and he would suffer from that extinction, because I suspect him of some vanity. I don't mean vanity in the Solomonian sense. Of all my people he's the one that has never been a vexation to my spirit. A most discreet, understanding man. ⟨. . .⟩

Heart of Darkness also received a certain amount of notice from the first; and of its origins this much may be said: it is well known that curious men go prying into all sorts of places (where they have no business) and come out of them with all kinds of spoil. This story, and one other, not in this volume, are all the spoil I brought out from the centre of Africa, where, really, I had no sort of business. More ambitious in its scope and longer in the telling, *Heart of Darkness* is quite as authentic in fundamentals as 'Youth.' It is, obviously, written in another mood, I won't characterize the mood precisely, but anybody can see that it is anything but the mood of wistful regret, of reminiscent tenderness.

—Joseph Conrad, Introduction to *Youth* (1917), *Conrad's Prefaces to His Works* (London: J. M. Dent & Sons, 1937): pp. 71–73.

LEONARD F. DEAN ON THE WEAK ENDING OF THE STORY

[Leonard F. Dean was a professor of English at New York University from 1967 until his retirement in 1975. A leading Shakespeare critic, he wrote *The Play of Language* (1970) and edited *A Casebook on Othello* (1961). Here he outlines the deficiencies in the story's ending.]

The conclusion of "The Heart of Darkness" produces a far different effect, although the intention is the same. The symbolism is melodramatic. The Intended has not earned the quality which she is meant to represent, and her effect is further weakened by the Hollywood set in which she is placed. When she extends her arms, the pose and the calculated manipulation of light, shadow, and black drapery recall too obviously the earlier mechanical symbol of the savage queen on the banks of the Congo. These lapses may be explained in part by reference to limitations in Conrad's artistic resources. The conclusion of the story, unlike the Congo experiences, was probably invented. Conrad's weakness in invention has often been noticed. It is implied by his preoccupation with the importance of reading symbolic meaning into actual experience. A wider explanation, however, is to be reached through a study of his use of Marlow. This fictitious narrator is usually explained as a device for securing aesthetic distance between the reader and the plot, thus reducing the impact of Conrad's romantic material. In

"The Heart of Darkness" Marlow does serve to interest us in meaning rather than in brute action, but he also prevents Conrad and the reader from fully experiencing the final tragic effect. It is Marlow rather than Kurtz who returns to affirm his faith in the Intended. This is unsatisfactory because Marlow has only observed Kurtz's horror. His somewhat parallel sickness is an inadequate substitute for Kurtz's complete disillusionment. In fact, Marlow's moral insight appears to be nearly as penetrating at the beginning of his journey as at the end. It was perhaps inevitable, given his artistic function, that he should be a static character.

—Leonard F. Dean, "Tragic Pattern in Conrad's 'Heart of Darkness,'" *College English* 6, no. 2 (November 1944): pp. 103–4.

ALBERT J. GUÉRARD ON THE STORY'S TRUE FOCUS

[Albert J. Guérard, a former professor of English at Stanford University, is the author of many books, including *André Gide* (1951) and *The Triumph of the Novel: Dickens, Dostoevsky, Faulkner* (1976). Here he explains that the story's central concern is Marlow's exploration of himself.]

It is time to recognize that the story *Heart of Darkness* is not primarily about Kurtz or about the brutality of Belgian officials but about Marlow its narrator. To what extent it also expresses the Joseph Conrad a biographer might conceivably recover, who in 1898 still felt a debt must be paid for his Congo journey and who paid it by the writing of this story, is doubtless an insoluble question. I suspect two facts (of a possible several hundred) are important. First, that going to the Congo was the enactment of a childhood wish associated with the disapproved childhood ambition to go to sea, and that this belated enactment was itself profoundly disapproved, in 1890, by the uncle and guardian. It was another gesture of a man bent on throwing his life away. But even more important may be the guilt of complicity, just such a guilt as many novelists of the Second World War have been obliged to work off. What Conrad thought of the expedition of the Katanga Company of 1890–1892 is accurately reflected in his remarks on the "Eldorado Exploring Expedition" of "Heart of Darkness": "It was reckless without hardihood, greedy without audacity, and cruel without courage . . . with no more moral purpose at the back of it than there is in burglars breaking into a safe." Yet Conrad hoped to obtain command of the expedition's ship even after he had returned from the initiatory voyage dramatized in his novel. Thus the adventurous Conrad and Conrad the moralist may have experienced collision. But the collision, again as with so many novelists of the second war, could well have been deferred and retrospective, not felt intensely at the time.

So much for the elusive Conrad of the biographers and of the "Congo Diary." Substantially and in its central emphasis "Heart of Darkness" concerns Marlow (projection to whatever great or small degree of a more irrecoverable Conrad) and his journey toward and through certain facets or potentialities of self. F. R. Leavis seems to regard him as a narrator only, providing a "specific and concretely realized point of view." But Marlow reiterates often enough that he is recounting a spiritual voyage of self-discovery. He remarks casually but crucially that he did not know himself before setting out, and that he likes work for the chance it provides to "find yourself . . . what no other man can ever know." The Inner Station "was the farthest point of navigation and the culminating point of my experience." At a material and rather superficial level, the journey is through the temptation of atavism. It is a record of "remote kinship" with the "wild and passionate uproar," of a "trace of a response" to it, of a final rejection of the "fascination of the abomination." And why should there not be the trace of a response? "The mind of man is capable of anything—because everything is in it, all the past as well as all the future." Marlow's temptation is made concrete through his exposure to Kurtz, a white man and sometime idealist who had fully responded to the wilderness: a potential and fallen self. "I had turned to the wilderness really, not to Mr. Kurtz." At the climax Marlow follows Kurtz ashore, confounds the beat of the drum with the beating of his heart, goes through the ordeal of looking into Kurtz's "mad soul," and brings him back to the ship. He returns to Europe a changed and more knowing man. Ordinary people are now "intruders whose knowledge of life was to me an irritating pretence, because I felt so sure they could not possibly know the things I knew."

On this literal plane, and when the events are so abstracted from the dream-sensation conveying them, it is hard to take Marlow's plight very seriously. Will he, the busy captain and moralizing narrator, also revert to savagery, go ashore for a howl and a dance, indulge unspeakable lusts? The late Victorian reader (and possibly Conrad himself) could take this more seriously than we; could literally believe not merely in a Kurtz's deterioration through months of solitude but also in the sudden reversions to the "beast" of naturalistic fiction. Insofar as Conrad does want us to take it seriously and literally, we must admit the nominal triumph of a currently accepted but false psychology over his own truer intuitions. But the triumph is only nominal. For the personal narrative is unmistakably authentic, which means that it explores something truer, more fundamental, and distinctly less material: the night journey into the unconscious, and confrontation of an entity within the self. "I flung one shoe overboard, and became aware that that was exactly what I had been looking forward to—a talk with Kurtz." It little matters what, in terms of psychological symbolism, we call this double or say he represents: whether the Freudian id or the Jungian shadow or more vaguely the outlaw. And I am afraid it is impossible to say where Conrad's conscious understanding of his story began and ended. The important thing is that the introspective plunge and powerful dream seem true; and are therefore inevitably moving.

—Albert J. Guérard, *Conrad the Novelist* (Cambridge: Harvard University Press, 1958): pp. 37–39.

LIONEL TRILLING ON THE STORY'S DISTURBING AMBIVALENCE TOWARD CIVILIZATION

Lionel Trilling (1905–1975) was a professor of literature at Columbia University for more than 44 years. His works of criticism include *The Liberal Imagination, Sincerity and Authenticity,* and *Mind in the Modern World.* He also wrote short stories, a novel, and several studies of Freud. Here he says one of the great strengths of the story is that the jungle is attractive not because of its freedom and purity but because it is "base and sordid."]

Whether or not Joseph Conrad read either Blake or Nietzsche I do not know, but his *Heart of Darkness* follows in their line. This very great work has never lacked for the admiration it deserves, and it has been given a kind of canonical place in the legend of modern literature by Eliot's having it so clearly in mind when he wrote *The Waste Land* and his having taken from it the epigraph to "The Hollow Men." But no one, to my knowledge, has ever confronted in an explicit way its strange and terrible message of ambivalence toward the life of civilization. Consider that its protagonist Kurtz is a progressive and a liberal and that he is the highly respected representative of a society which undertakes to represent itself as benign, although in fact it is vicious. Consider too that he is a practitioner of several arts, a painter, a writer, a musician, and into the bargain a political orator. He is at once the most idealistic and the most practically successful of all the agents of the Belgian exploitation of the Congo. Everybody knows what truth about him Marlow discovers—that Kurtz's success is the result of a terrible ascendancy he has gained over the natives of his distant station, an ascendancy which is derived from his presumed magical or divine powers, that he has exercised his rule with the extreme of cruelty, that he has given himself to unnamable acts of lust. This is the world of the darker pages of *The Golden Bough*. It is one of the great points of Conrad's story that Marlow speaks of the primitive life of the jungle not as being noble or charming or even free but as being base and sordid—and for *that* reason compelling: he himself feels quite overtly its dreadful attraction. It is to this devilish baseness that Kurtz has yielded himself, and yet Marlow, although he does indeed treat him with hostile irony, does not find it possible to suppose that Kurtz is anything but a hero of the spirit. For me it is still ambiguous whether Kurtz's famous deathbed cry, "The horror! The horror!" refers to the approach of death or to his experience of savage life. Whichever it is, to Marlow the fact that Kurtz could utter this cry at the point of death, while Marlow himself, when death threatens him, can know it only as a weary greyness, marks the difference between the ordinary man and a hero of the spirit. Is this not the essence of the modern belief about the nature of the artist, the man who goes down into that hell which is the historical beginning of the human soul, a beginning not outgrown but established in humanity as we know it now, preferring the reality of this hell to the bland lies of the civilization that has overlaid it?

—Lionel Trilling, "On the Modern Element in Modern Literature," *Partisan Review* 28, no. 1 (January/February 1961): pp. 25–26.

V. S. Naipaul Explains Why He Values Conrad

[V. S. Naipaul is a Trinidadian novelist, travel writer, and essayist. His many works include *An Area of Darkness, A Flag on the Island,* and *In a Free State.* This extract is taken from a essay that was read at the University of Kent at Canterbury on the fiftieth anniversary of Conrad's death. In it Naipaul describes the power of Conrad's "scrupulous fidelity to the truth of my own sensations."]

"An Outpost of Progress" is now to me the finest thing Conrad wrote. It is the story of two commonplace Belgians, new to the new Belgian Congo, who find that they have unwittingly, through their Negro assistant, traded Africans for ivory, are then abandoned by the surrounding tribesmen, and go mad. But my first judgment of it had been only literary. It had seemed familiar; I had read other stories of lonely white men going mad in hot countries. And my rediscovery, or discovery, of Conrad really began with one small scene in *Heart of Darkness.*

The African background—"the demoralized land" of plunder and licensed cruelty—I took for granted. That is how we can be imprisoned by our assumptions. The background now seems to me to be the most effective part of the book; but then it was no more than what I expected. The story of Kurtz, the up-river ivory agent, who is led to primitives and lunacy by his unlimited power over primitive men, was lost on me. But there was a page which spoke directly to me, and not only of Africa.

The steamer is going up river to meet Kurtz; it is "like travelling back to the earliest beginnings of the world." A hut is sighted on the bank. It is empty, but it contains one book, sixty years old, *An Inquiry into Some Points of Seamanship,* tattered, without covers, but "lovingly stitched afresh with white cotton thread." And in the midst of nightmare, this old book, "dreary . . . with illustrative diagrams and repulsive tables of figures," but with its "singleness of intention," its "honest concern for the right way of going to work," seems to the narrator to be "luminous with another than a professional light."

This scene, perhaps because I have carried it for so long, or perhaps because I am more receptive to the rest of the story, now makes less of an impression. But I suppose that at the time it answered something of the political panic I was beginning to feel.

To be a colonial was to know a kind of security; it was to inhabit a fixed world. And I suppose that in my fantasy I had seen myself coming to England as to some purely literary region, where, untrammelled by the accidents of history or background, I could make a romantic career for myself as a writer. But in the new world I felt the ground move below me. The new politics, the curious reliance of men on institutions they were yet working to undermine, the simplicity of beliefs and the hideous simplicity of actions, the corruption of causes, half-made societies that seemed doomed to remain half-made: these were the things that began to preoccupy me. They were not things from which I could detach myself. And I found that Conrad—sixty years before, in the time of a great peace—had been everywhere before me. Not as a man with a cause, but a man offering, as in *Nostromo,* a vision of the world's half-made societies as places which continuously made and unmade themselves, where there was no goal, and where always "something inherent in the necessities of successful action . . . carried with it the moral degradation of the idea." Dismal, but deeply felt: a kind of truth and half a consolation.

To understand Conrad, then, it was necessary to begin to match his experience. It was also necessary to lose one's preconceptions of what the novel should do and, above all, to rid oneself of the subtle corruptions of the novel or comedy of manners. When art copies life, and life in its turn mimics art, a writer's originality can often be obscured. ⟨. . .⟩

Conrad's value to me is that he is someone who sixty to seventy years ago meditated on my world, a world I recognize today. I feel this about no other writer of the century. His achievement derives from the honesty which is part of his difficulty, that "scrupulous fidelity to the truth of my own sensations."

Nothing is rigged in Conrad. He doesn't remake countries. He chose, as we now know, incidents from real life; and he meditated on them. "Meditate" is his own, exact word. And what he says about his heroine in *Nostromo* can be applied to himself. "The wisdom of the heart having no concern with the erection or demolition of theories any more than with the defense of prejudices, has no random words at its command. The words it pronounces have the value of acts of integrity, tolerance, and compassion."

—V. S. Naipaul, "Conrad's Darkness," *The New York Review of Books* 21, no. 16 (17 October 1974): pp. 17–18, 19.

CHINUA ACHEBE DENOUNCES CONRAD AS "A PURVEYOR OF COMFORTING MYTHS"

[Chinua Achebe, a distinguished Nigerian novelist, is a professor emeritus at the University of Nigeria. Among his best-known novels are *Things Fall Apart* (1958) and *A Man of the People* (1966). In this extract, Achebe argues that Conrad underhandedly contrasts Africa with the enlightened Western civilization.]

Heart of Darkness projects the image of Africa as "the other world," the antithesis of Europe and therefore of civilization, a place where a man's vaunted intelligence and refinement are finally mocked by triumphant bestiality. The book opens on the River Thames, tranquil, resting peacefully "at the decline of day after ages of good service done to the race that peopled its banks." But the actual story takes place on the River Congo, the very antithesis of the Thames. The River Congo is quite decidedly not a River Emeritus. It has rendered no service and enjoys no old-age pension. We are told that "going up that river was like travelling back to the earliest beginning of the world."

Is Conrad saying then that these two rivers are very different, one good, the other bad? Yes, but that is not the real point. What actually worries Conrad is the lurking hint of kinship, of common ancestry. For the Thames, too, "has been one of the dark places of the earth." It conquered its darkness, of course, and is now at peace. But if it were to visit its primordial relative, the Congo, it would run the terrible risk of hearing grotesque, suggestive echoes of its own forgotten darkness, and of falling victim to an avenging recrudescence of the mindless frenzy of the first beginnings.

I am not going to waste your time with examples of Conrad's famed evocation of the African atmosphere. In the final consideration it amounts to no more than a steady, ponderous, fake-ritualistic repetition of two sentences, one about silence and the other about frenzy. An example of the former is "It was the stillness of an implacable force brooding over an inscrutable intention" and of the latter, "The steamer toiled along slowly on the edge of a black and incomprehensible frenzy." Of course, there is a judicious change of adjective from time to time so that instead of "inscrutable," for example, you might have "unspeakable," etc., etc.

The eagle-eyed English critic F. R. Leavis drew attention nearly thirty years ago to Conrad's "adjectival insistence upon inexpressible and incomprehensible mystery." That insistence must not be dismissed lightly, as many Conrad critics have tended to do, as a mere stylistic flaw. For it raises serious questions of artistic good faith. When a writer, while pretending to record scenes, incidents and their impact, is in reality engaged in inducing hypnotic stupor in his readers through a bombardment of emotive words and other forms of trickery much more has to be at stake than stylistic felicity. Generally, normal readers are well armed to detect and resist such underhand activity. But Conrad chose his subject well—one which was guaranteed not to put him in conflict with the psychological predisposition of his readers or raise the need for him to contend with their resistance. He chose the role of purveyor of comforting myths.

The most interesting and revealing passages in *Heart of Darkness* are, however, about people. I must quote a long passage from the middle of the story in which representatives of Europe in a steamer going down the Congo encounter the denizens of Africa:

> We were wanderers on a prehistoric earth, on an earth that wore the aspect of an unknown planet. We could have fancied ourselves the first of men taking possession of an accursed inheritance, to be subdued at the cost of profound anguish and of excessive toil. But suddenly, as we struggled round a bend, there would be a glimpse of rush walls, of peaked grass-roofs, a burst of yells, a whirl of black limbs, a mass of hands clapping, of feet stamping, of bodies swaying, of eyes rolling, under the droop of heavy and motionless foliage. The steamer toiled along slowly on the edge of a black and incomprehensible frenzy. The prehistoric man was cursing us, praying to us, welcoming us—who could tell? We were cut off from the comprehension of our surroundings; we glided past like phantoms, wondering and secretly appalled, as sane men would be before an enthusiastic outbreak in a madhouse. We could not remember because we were travelling in the night of first ages, of those ages that are gone, leaving hardly a sign—and no memories.
>
> The earth seemed unearthly. We are accustomed to look upon the shackled form of a conquered monster, but there—there you could look at a thing monstrous and free. It was unearthly, and the men were—No, they were not inhuman. Well, you know, that was the worst of it—this suspicion of their not being inhuman. It would come slowly to one. They howled and leaped, and spun, and made horrid faces; but what thrilled you was just the thought of your remote kinship with this wild and passionate uproar. Ugly. Yes, it was ugly enough; but if you were man enough you would admit to yourself

that there was in you just the faintest trace of a response to the terrible frankness of that noise, a dim suspicion of there being a meaning in it which you—you so remote from the night of first ages—could comprehend.

Herein lies the meaning of *Heart of Darkness* and the fascination it holds over the Western mind: "What thrilled you was just the thought of their humanity—like yours. . . . Ugly."

—Chinua Achebe, "An Image of Africa," *Massachusetts Review* 18, no. 4 (Winter 1977): pp. 783–85.

SURESH RAVAL ON MARLOW'S TURMOIL

[Suresh Raval is a professor of English at the University of Arizona. Here he explains how Marlow is destroyed when he realizes that values can provide no redemption.]

Marlow, in his seemingly reposeful posture of a Buddha, is not an exemplary figure of detachment and moral calm that the image of the Buddha may suggest. His inner turmoil sharply differentiates him from the Buddha of ancient India whose reposeful calm is the result of his renunciation of this world of ceaseless toil and acquisition, suffering and death. Marlow's turmoil marks him as a representative of Western culture; he has not renounced the world, but has believed in the redeeming possibility of values, and is shattered by their absence. Hence his words: "It was not my strength that wanted nursing, it was my imagination that wanted soothing." If morality originates in the fear of violence, if the police and the butcher must restrain the self that cannot autonomously restrain itself, there can be no absolute redemptive value in morality, self, or work. After such disillusionment one cannot seek foundations for morality. Marlow's moral will can claim to alter nothing, though it can narrate the events that form the basis of his experience.

Thus a reading of *Heart of Darkness* which places Marlow close to Socrates and distant, say, from Sartre ignores those elements in Socrates which lead to an unmasking of actual life. Moreover, as

Nietzsche argued, Socrates undermined the foundations of practical life in classical Athens. Marlow's narrative takes on neither a Socratic nor a Sartrean configuration; it is composed of dramatic moments that complicate Socratic or Sartrean perspectives. The Socratic view, in any case, would be that Kurtz is foolhardy rather than courageous, belligerent and unreliable rather than wise and good. For Socrates insisted the brave man considers only the good life worth living. Kurtz has, in this view, capitulated to base impulses which render his courage reckless and self-destructive. ⟨. . .⟩

Marlow's act of storytelling, however, does involve a commitment to preserve the truth of experience, though it is a commitment devoid of conventional piety or hope. In this sense Marlow may be said to have evolved a self beyond culture, a self that knows the awesome terrors held at bay by its awesome will to be human. It is here that Lionel Trilling's idea that the highest value of a culture is in its capacity to create the possibility of a self that exists apart from and beyond culture seems relevant. But there is in a sense no such thing as "self" beyond culture. Culture here means the context of historically developed social practices which helps create the possibility of a self. This self, in so far as it is founded on ideals, is impossible to realize in practice; thus it generates restraints which protect against transgressions that damage the social well-being. Having known Kurtz in his extremity, Marlow has come to see the self as an arbitrary construct, rather than one created by transcendental values. Thus Marlow is a representative of Western culture who is distanced from that culture's grandest claims about itself; he is utterly devoid of confidence. This is why he says: "life is a greater riddle than some of us think it to be. I was within a hair's breadth of the last opportunity for pronouncement, and I found with humiliation that probably I would have nothing to say." His speech culminates in silence.

Marlow's "self", however, cannot be institutionalized, for to believe that it can be would be to ascribe to human beings unlimited capacity to bear the truth. One cannot forget the moral force of the lie to the Intended or her tragic sanity. One cannot imagine the Russian harlequin learning from experience, or the manager and the pilgrims living lives of moral pessimism that comprehends and endures the nihilism pervasive in our social-political institutions. Neither can one hope to redeem the idealism whose moral complicity with imperialism *Heart of Darkness* delineates with such brilliance.

—Suresh Raval, *The Art of Failure* (Boston: Allen & Unwin, 1986): pp. 42–44.

RUTH L. NADELHAFT ON CONRAD'S CONTRADICTORY VIEWS ON WOMEN

[Ruth L. Nadelhaft is a professor of English at the University of Maine. In this extract she describes Conrad's conflicting use of women, as well as Marlow's perspective that they are larger than life.]

Heart of Darkness contains several kinds of women, several kinds of perspectives, testifying to Conrad's unfixed, even conflicting sense of what roles women must play both in his fiction and in the world of imperialism which is his subject.

In some respects, the enigmatic women who serve as the gate-keepers of the company office in Brussels offer the most schematic view of women as mythic powers, at home in a world deeper and more permanent than the crowded and competitive marketplace in which Charlie Marlow competes for his livelihood. Their profound understanding expresses itself through their silent manipulation of the forms of business; though 'plain as an umbrella-cover' in dress, each woman 'seemed to know all about them and about me too. . . . She seemed uncanny and fateful.' Yet, within two pages of text, Marlow breezily comments, 'It's queer how out of touch women are. They live in a world of their own, and there has never been anything like it, and never can be.' This abrupt contradiction has usually been ignored by Conradian critics. ⟨. . .⟩

Virtually all criticism concerned with *Heart of Darkness* attempts to exonerate or explain away Marlow's lie to the Intended—not because it diminishes her but because, as Marlow worries, such a lie suggests his failure to live up to the ferocious example of Kurtz, to the man who faces the ultimate truth about himself and his relation to the universe. Marlow's concern is to do 'justice' to Kurtz, and his halting conversation with Kurtz's Intended serves primarily to expose her insularity and idealisation of her lover. With increasing sarcasm, Marlow echoes and encourages her adulation of Kurtz until he speaks out of a 'dull anger' and finds himself confronted by her desperate request for Kurtz's last words.

What needs explaining in that last section of the tale is not so much the technical lie to the Intended, the substitution of her name for 'the horror, the horror', but Marlow's sardonic and manipulative treatment of the woman from the first moments of their meeting. Indeed, Marlow's barely concealed hostility arises as the Intended ascribes to him love and friendship towards Kurtz. "'He drew men towards him by what was best in them'", she says. "'It is the gift of the great.'" At this point, as at others in the scene, Marlow answers only obliquely; but his obliquity extends to his listeners as well as to Kurtz's Intended. For what this woman seems to penetrate, in her own darkness, is Marlow's weakness, Marlow's susceptibility to her own form of adulation. ⟨. . .⟩

In his retaliatory manipulation of the conversation with Kurtz's Intended, Marlow brings to a rounded conclusion his attitudes towards women which have in many ways helped to determine his behaviour throughout this complex narrative. A man of anxious idealisation, one who finds it difficult to be indebted to a woman, given to the deprecation of the personal, Marlow from the outset wrestles with the provocations of women. Whether as emblems of material or sexual power, the women of this story, seen through the language of the narrator, emerge as larger than life.

—Ruth L. Nadelhaft, *Joseph Conrad* (Atlantic Highlands, N.J.: Humanities Press International, 1991): pp. 46, 48–49.

JOYCE CAROL OATES ON THE COEXISTENCE OF GOOD AND EVIL

[Joyce Carol Oates is the Roger S. Berlind Distinguished Professor in the Humanities at Princeton University. She is a Pulitzer Prize nominee who has written numerous novels and collections of short stories, poetry, and plays. Here she describes Conrad's desire for Kurtz to be seen as a tragic hero.]

Joseph Conrad's "Heart of Darkness," though elaborately composed of oscillating images of light and dark, order and chaos, is by far the most realistic of these unusual works of fiction ⟨*Dr. Jekyll and Mr. Hyde, The Picture of Dorian Gray,* and *The Turn of the Screw*⟩; yet here, too, is a powerful mythic portrait of a "good" man, Kurtz (the chief of the inner station of the trading company, "an emissary of pity, and science, and progress, and devil knows what else"), who is simultaneously an "evil" man (a vicious, unscrupulous trader in ivory who ends up tyrannizing African natives, his jungle sanctuary surrounded by the grisly emblems of his madness, the decapitated heads of native "enemies"). Kurtz, whom Marlow had sought avidly, risking his own life in a treacherous and foolhardy adventure that comes close to destroying him, is both Dr. Jekyll and Mr. Hyde; the elixir that fatally releases his primitive, evil self is simply distance from home, the freedom of a white man's power over those whom he considers his racial "inferiors," whose influence over him is sub-liminal and unacknowledged. ⟨. . .⟩

It is Marlow's compelling argument, and through Marlow Conrad's, that the mind of man is capable of anything "because everything is in it, all the past as well as all the future." Marlow's (and Conrad's) journey up the Congo is, in one sense, a journey back into time: beginning with Marlow's apprehension that England, too, was once "one of the dark places of the earth" and moving to a consider-ation of the "fascination of the abomination"—the fascination of civilized man for his primitive, atavistic roots. What romance there is in Conrad's prose, in his celebration of such truths: "The voice of the surf heard now and then was a positive pleasure, like the speech of a brother." ⟨. . .⟩

The anxieties aroused by Charles Darwin's controversial, bitterly contested theory of evolution by way of natural selection, first pro-mulgated in *Origin of Species* (1859) and subsequently in *The Descent of Man* (1871) are given tragic dramatic form in the tale of Kurtz's deterioration in the jungle, the much-acclaimed Kurtz of whom it is said by Marlow that "all of Europe had gone into [his] making." Conrad's irony is a constant throughout the narrative, like a haunting vibration beyond the sounds of words normally uttered. And what intransigent irony in Kurtz's final words, as if Shakespeare's unregenerate Edmund, or Iago, and not Lear or Othello, were the touchstones of moral truth. Dying of fever in the jungle, as Marlow nearly dies, Kurtz's famous pronouncement of his own spiritual condition—"The horror! The horror!"—is a judgment upon man's universal propensity for evil. What is this mysterious kinship that Marlow feels with the doomed man, whom he has traveled hundreds of miles to meet, only to discover him moribund, hideous? "It was as if an animated image of death carved out of old ivory had been shaking its hand with menaces at a motionless crowd of men made of dark and glittering bronze." (Compare Marlow's subterranean connection with Kurtz to the idealized and romanticized connection between the immature young captain of "The Secret Sharer" and his double, the fugitive Leggatt.) ⟨. . .⟩

Through the prism of shimmering, musical language that is the essence of Conrad's achievement in "Heart of Darkness," the author has hoped to elevate Kurtz, a white racist murderer whose actions have parodied the idealism of his speech, to the stature of tragedy; he is one whose degradation at the end of his life can't be the sole measure of his moral worth.

—Joyce Carol Oates, Introduction to *Heart of Darkness and The Secret Sharer* (New York: Signet Classic, 1997): pp. 2, 3–4, 5.

CEDRIC WATTS ON CONRAD'S BOLD RADICALISM

[Cedric Watts is a professor of English at the University of Sussex. The author of *Joseph Conrad: A Literary Life* (1989), he also has written many other works on Conrad, as well as books on Shakespeare and Thomas Hardy. He edited *Joseph Conrad's Letters to R. B. Cunninghame Graham* (1969), as well as many of Conrad's works. Here he explains that the striking originality of "Heart of Darkness" lies not just in its technique but also in its subject matter, which critically confronts problems that would persist into the late twentieth century.]

'Heart of Darkness' is supreme among Conrad's *novelle* or longer tales. It is exciting and profound, lucid and bewildering; highly compressed, immensely rich in texture and implication; and it has a recessive adroitness, for its paradoxes repeatedly ambush the conceptualizing reader or critic. Thematically it holds a remarkably wide range of reference to problems of politics and psychology, morality and religion, social order and evolution. The narrative dextrously embodies literary theories which were yet to be formulated: defamiliarization, deconstructionism, delayed decoding, covert plotting. 'Heart of Darkness' can be related to a diversity of traditions, generic and technical, including political satire, protest literature, traveller's tale, psychological odyssey, symbolic novel, mediated autobiography; while, to those readers who seek prophecies, it speaks eloquently of the brutalities and follies of subsequent history. As was demonstrated by Coppola's film *Apocalypse Now* (1979), this tale about Africa in 1890 entailed, among many other possibilities, a sardonic commentary on the Vietnam war of the 1970s. In its techniques and tentacular implications, 'Heart of Darkness' is often so boldly and intelligently radical that this Victorian narrative generates the procedures of Modernism and critically confronts some major problems of life in the twentieth century.

As in 'Youth', the tale uses doubly oblique narration: an anonymous character reports the story told by Marlow. This time, however, the oblique narrative technique is used much more searchingly, so that one of the main co-ordinators of the story is the linguistic theme, which emphasizes not only the difficulty of communicating truly what is obscure or profound but also the attractions and perils of charismatic eloquence. Indeed, one of the many paradoxes of 'Heart of Darkness' is that this narrative offers eloquent warnings about eloquence, while effectively communicating the difficulty of effective communication. An important political aspect of this theme is displayed by the tale's demonstration that there is an imperialism of discourse which both licenses and conceals the excesses of economic exploitation. The generative and transformative relationship of language to the world is made problematically evident.

The sophistication, compression, and obliquities of the tale are such that it needs to be read several times to be adequately comprehended. At a first reading many ironies are likely to pass unnoticed. We may not see, for instance, that Marlow's initial descriptions of the Roman trireme-commander and the 'decent young citizen in a toga' offer ironic counterparts to Marlow himself and Kurtz in Africa; nor may we see that the tale has a 'covert murder plot', in which the manager schemes to destroy the ailing Kurtz by delaying the steamer which is supposed to relieve Kurtz's outpost. Certainly the satiric indictment of colonialism in Africa is graphically clear at first reading, as is the mockery of the myopic arrogance of Europeans in daring to impose themselves on alien territory. Many of the 'pilgrims' function as mere avaricious automata; and as for Kurtz himself, who brought idealistic ambitions to the wilderness, he proves to be depraved and deranged. In its cumulation of images of absurdity, of savage farce, of wanton destruction and demented energy, 'Heart of Darkness' can seem a fiercely pessimistic narrative. Its positive values lie partly in the quality of civilization represented by Marlow, who usually preserves a vigilant humanity; they lie largely in the authorial indignation at man's inhumanity to man and, indeed, at the despoliation of the earth in the name of 'progress'; and they are richly implicit in the articulate intelligence, sensitivity, and exuberance of the text. ⟨. . .⟩

The Kurtzes of the world may often make its history; the Marlows of the world provide its conscience.

—Cedric Watts, Introduction to *Heart of Darkness and Other Tales* (Oxford: Oxford University Press, 1998): pp. xiv–xvi, xxiii.

Plot Summary of
"The Secret Sharer"

"I wondered how far I should turn out faithful to that ideal conception of one's own personality every man sets up for himself secretly." So ponders the narrator at the opening of "The Secret Sharer," rather neatly drawing the reader's attention to one of the story's most basic issues. The narrator is a new captain, not only because this is his first command but also because he has only been appointed to this ship a fortnight before, although his crew has been together for at least eighteen months. The neophyte also is nearly the youngest man on board. The ship is anchored at the head of the Gulf of Siam.

The captain tells his first mate that he will stay on deck himself for the anchor watch until one o'clock or so. He knows the sailors are tired, having worked very hard the previous few days. His "strangeness" makes him sleepless, and he also wants to explore his ship on his own. The move is an odd one, he knows, and he hears the second mate's incredulous response when the first mate leaves and tells him the news.

While walking the deck, the captain notices a rope ladder left hanging over the ship's side and upon reaching to pull it in is surprised that he cannot get it to budge. He leans over and sees one arm draped on the lowest ladder rung. When this swimmer, named Leggatt, hears he is talking to the captain, he explains that he has been in the water a long time, climbs the ladder, and is offered an extra sleeping suit of the captain's, which fits him exactly.

He follows the captain "like my double" to a light on deck and says he was the first mate on the *Sephora*, a Liverpool vessel anchored nearby. The reader learns that Leggatt had attended the same training school as the narrator, and that his father is a parson on Norfolk. He also admits that he has killed a man, and tells the captain that he believes a judge and jury won't be lenient in his case. The captain listens to his description of how the murder happened some weeks ago, never questioning its truth and feeling "as though I were myself inside that other sleeping suit."

The *Sephora* had been caught in a terrible storm, and the men were in the midst of trying to set up a reefed foresail after their main topsail had blown away, when Leggatt was given a hard time by one of the men, a man he says was miserable and wicked. The two ended up in a fight, Leggatt had him by the throat, and then a huge wave landed on them on deck. When it cleared, Leggatt was still holding the now-dead man by the throat. The captain of the *Sephora* and the rest of the crew started screaming that Leggatt was a murderer. He was relieved of his duties and locked up for nearly seven weeks in his cabin.

After hearing this tale, the narrator brings Leggatt into his stateroom, which, due to its L-shaped layout, makes it not so easy to see into the whole room upon entering. So begins the hiding of Leggatt, which places an increasing strain on the captain. He tells the reader that Leggatt is "not a bit like me, really." Yet the man, apparently, is some part of himself that he must come to terms with, a man who can kill someone, who can carry out a daring escape, who can remain unruffled, yet who also runs from his punishment.

Immediately in the morning we see that the secrecy is difficult for the captain. He jumps and barks at the steward bringing his coffee, and again when the steward warns him to close his port, and then again when the steward, by this time standing hesitantly in the doorway, asks if he can retrieve the now-empty coffee cup.When the captain goes on deck, he sees the steward talking to his officers and knows the steward has told them something of the recent incidents in his cabin. The captain and his officers have breakfast, and he is frigid with fear, knowing his stowaway is just behind the door that faces him as he sits at the head of the table. "It was very much like being mad, only it was worse because one was aware of it."

The fear intensifies when the captain hears that the *Sephora*'s captain is heading toward them in a small boat. He has just been looking for Leggatt on the nearby islands. The *Sephora*'s captain, whose name is something like Archbold, is brought into the narrator's room. He retells the story Leggatt has told, but with a twist: Archbold says that he, not Leggatt, was the one who gave the command to set up the foresail. The narrator asks him if the heavy wave might have actually killed the man on board, but the captain responds negatively. Archbold then reveals that he never liked Leggatt, even though he looks very smart and gentlemanly, for he himself is a plain man. He says he will have to write to his owners that Leggatt has committed suicide.

The captain starts to feel that Archbold distrusts him, not only because he reminds Archbold of Leggatt but because the captain doesn't seem thoroughly intrigued by Archbold's story. In response, the captain forcefully starts flinging open doors, not just within his own accommodations but throughout the ship. After Archbold finally leaves, close calls continue, and the captain feels he is nearly insane. He sees his first mate talking to other crew members and motioning about his craziness.

In a private moment, Leggatt tells the captain that he must maroon him on a nearby island. The captain shortly realizes the idea is right, and Leggatt voices his thoughts, explaining: "It's a great satisfaction to have got somebody to understand. . . . It's very wonderful." At midnight the captain goes up on deck and orders the ship to turn, at which the mate is most surprised, his whiskers twitching "in silent criticism." The whiskers flail around even more when the captain announces he will move close to the islands to find a breeze. Then the mate questions him, in shock at the idea of getting so close to reefs and shoals.

When the captain explains to Leggatt that they will move in by the island of Koh-ring because it seems like it must be inhabited, he realizes for the first time that his own future might be destroyed if he makes a terrible mistake on his first command. He explains to Leggatt how to get off the ship and wraps three gold pieces in a handkerchief around Leggatt's waist, sticking his own floppy hat on his head at the last moment to protect him from the fierce island heat. Back up on deck he is shocked at how close they already are to the island but persists in bringing the ship even more dangerously close. The ship is silent, with all men on deck, and as the first mate loses control the captain grabs his arm to keep him from smacking his head. The captain holds on and shakes, recalling Leggatt's grip on the mutinous man he strangled.

Finally the captain forgets about his double and thinks of how he is a stranger to his own ship, not knowing her capabilities. He realizes that since he doesn't know her feel that he cannot even tell if she is still moving and wishes he had a piece of paper to throw in the water so he could note its reaction. Just at this moment, he sees his own floppy hat floating right near the ship. The hat had been meant to protect his friend, but now it is saving his ship. He sees that it is drifting forward, warning him just in time, and orders that the ship be turned. The men are no longer quiet but relieved and then thrilled, following the first mate's orders for pulling the ship out of danger "with a great noise, amidst cheery cries." The captain feels at one with his ship and catches a glimpse of his hat, marking the spot where his secret friend first lowered himself into the water and a new life. ✸

List of Characters in
"The Secret Sharer"

The *captain* is the story's narrator. He is new to the ship and is nearly the youngest man on board. This is his first command.

Leggatt is the former first mate of the *Sephora* who has killed a man. He is no more than twenty-five, with "regular" features, light eyes, and a small brown mustache. He is uncannily steady, calm, and sure.

The *chief mate* is one who enjoys puzzling over seeming mysteries. His "frightful" whiskers are what the captain notices most about him.

The *second mate* is the only man on board that is younger than the captain. He is quiet, willing to question the captain, yet easily subdued.

The *skipper* of the *Sephora* has been her captain for fifteen years and is well-known, having been at sea for thirty-seven years. He has a name the narrator says he cannot remember with certainty, but he thinks it is something like Archbold. The narrator says his strongest trait is his "spiritless tenacity." He conforms to the rules. ❁

Critical Views on
"The Secret Sharer"

PAUL L. WILEY ON THE CAPTAIN'S BATTLE IN
FOLLOWING HIS PERSONAL CODE OF ETHICS

[Paul L. Wiley has been a professor of English at the University of Wisconsin and is the author of *Novelist of Three Worlds: Ford Madox Ford*. He describes in this extract the arduous consequences of the captain's decision to abide by his own morality instead of society's.]

The shock of discovering Leggatt swimming alone in the sea gives the Captain both visual proof that the world is not secure and also an image of that side of his own nature which is immersed in the same dark waters. In consequence he feels identified with Leggatt and accepts without hesitation the latter's story of having killed one of the crew of the *Sephora* under the stress of passion during a storm. Leggatt's danger thus conveys a warning not only of the Captain's own limitations, already glimpsed by the reader in the matter of the anchor watch, but also of the peril of self-idealization in a world hostile to ideals. This disclosure of the conflicting tendencies in man leads to the feeling of duality which brings the Captain near the point of madness. The psychological aspect of his dilemma merges with the moral problem of helping a man guilty of a crime according to social convention. In aiding Leggatt, he acts in accordance with necessity and with the instinct of sympathy; yet the partnership between the two men, which enables the Captain to obtain self-knowledge, also stands in the way of his approach to familiarity with his ship. His erratic behavior in keeping Leggatt concealed makes him suspect in the eyes of the crew.

This situation reaches a climax in the scene between the Captain and Archbold, the master of the *Sephora*, when the latter arrives in search of his missing captive. The alternatives before the Captain here are ⟨. . .⟩ to surrender Leggatt to punishment at the cost of human feeling or to protect him at the risk of the Captain's whole future. Archbold completes, therefore, the main triad of characters who figure in the allegory of conventional and private justice. He appears to represent a narrow creed of vengeance at variance with conditions in a world of accident. He seems to the Captain dull and tenacious in a spiritless way in his desire to turn Leggatt over to authority despite the fact that the mate's courageous performance during the storm has saved the ship:

> His obscure tenacity on that point had in it something incomprehensible and a little awful; something, as it were, mystical, quite apart from his anxiety that he should not be suspected of "countenancing any doings of that sort." Seven-and-thirty virtuous years at sea, of which over twenty of immaculate command, and the last fifteen in the *Sephora*, seemed to have laid him under some pitiless obligation.

Yet Archbold stands for the law on the *Sephora;* and in taking sides with Leggatt against him, the Captain disobeys a mandate of established legality in favor of a personal code which recognizes the common bond between men in their submission to error. The incident is timed expertly to occur at the moment when the Captain's efforts to hide Leggatt have strained his endurance to the utmost and thus to emphasize the full burden of choice that oppresses modern man caught in a state of divided loyalties. ⟨. . .⟩ The Captain comes to the verge of disaster in fulfilling his pact with Leggatt and in acquiring knowledge of human capacities for strength and weakness. Yet the hat which he gives Leggatt as a token of pity saves him and his ship under the shadows of Koh-Ring and marks his acceptance of the concrete fact that determines action.

—Paul L. Wiley, *Conrad's Measure of Man* (New York: Gordian Press, 1954): pp. 95–97.

EDWARD W. SAID ON HOW THE CAPTAIN IS DETERMINED NOT TO CHANGE

[Edward W. Said is Old Dominion Foundation Professor of Humanities at Columbia University. Among his many books are *Literature and Society* (1980) and *Culture and Imperialism* (1993). Here he takes issue with the critics that see the captain as a better man because of his encounter with Leggatt.]

Conrad has now established the sweep of his literary universe: he has question-begged away the process by which truth is corrupted into serviceable ideas by man's egoism. England and her closet of imagery have become his, shielding him from the heart of darkness. And it is precisely into this eminently British realm, inhabited with youthful discomposure by the narrator of "The Secret Sharer," that Conrad introduces Leggatt.

The challenge before the neophyte captain (whom I shall call X) is seen against an English background of "fair play" and innate racial superiority. His ideal conception of himself, he thinks, will have to be tried according to British tradition and the exigencies of Leggatt's difficult, but unmistakably British, presence. X's self-conscious effort to play his part is not only to keep Leggatt safe; he also wants to keep his activity within certain strategic restrictions. Together, the two young men threaten these restrictions by revealing their discontent with them. Leggatt shares X's unadmitted wish to escape from the notional, social, and philosophic prison in which for better or for worse X had, like Conrad, willfully placed himself. In order to attain goals that his prison does not allow, X must honestly ask himself the question: Am I able to realize my ideal of freedom by myself? The question is answered when X receives the man out of the dark, as a phosphorescent gleam of light emanating from the indifferent sea, and keeps him hidden on board as a temporary apostle of unrestricted freedom. X performs his risky concealment of the fugitive, but then goes no further. It is difficult to believe, as some critics have suggested, that X is a great deal better for his brief encounter with Leggatt. Leggatt simply increases X's confidence in the world of his previous choice. There is no probing of the idea because that idea "will not stand much looking into." Once X has no more use for Leggatt, Leggatt returns to the sea.

Just as a storm gains its full identity in the heart of the exemplary sailor who resists its attack, so Leggatt's presence on the ship endows X with an image of his secret self. But the image is both covert and strangely shameful. On his own ship, in bondage to its limited world, alienated from his crew, X uses Leggatt to gain an even more determined hold on himself as *he is*. The test of his 'ideal' view of himself returns X to the British world he knows best. In short, "The Secret Sharer" is a hortatory intellectual fable about why a tricky escape from so-called duty is not after all possible. The image of the double, and with it a plot that tests the hero, does not occasion the searching, profoundly serious self-examination that Marlow, say, undergoes in *Heart of Darkness*. Conrad chose what was certainly the easier treatment of the theme, perhaps because—as I have already suggested—by the time of "The Secret Sharer" he had exhausted himself in his own struggles with darkness. By seeing an image of himself in another person, X can ascertain his own identity and exert a tamer, less exacting assault upon his surroundings. When Leggatt swims off to a new destiny, there is a significant absence of further description of X's future. A letter from Conrad to Galsworthy of May 5, 1905, is especially revealing on this point:

> I own I expected good news from you. They are none the less welcome for that. I was more concerned than uneasy at your seediness, which I seemed to know so well. It was like beholding one's own weird acquaintance in a looking glass: my own well known mysterious, disturbing sensations reflected in your personality, which is as near the inner me as anything not absolutely myself can be. I saw you depart from Naples with a feeling of confidence that no usual current mistrust of life could qualify. You were going off in good hands. And I returned tranquil as to your fate—to the tortures of my awful, overwhelming indolence—the very negation of tranquility—just as a cage is not a shelter, is the negation of a place of rest.

If X is later to suffer like this, from indolence, we can be sure that it will be because he has lived in a cage that looks like a shelter.

—Edward W. Said, *Joseph Conrad and the Fiction of Autobiography* (Cambridge, Mass.: Harvard University Press, 1966): pp. 156–58.

H. M. DALESKI ON THE REAL NEED FOR BRINGING THE SHIP SO CLOSE TO SHORE

[H. M. Daleski has been a professor of English at the Hebrew University of Jerusalem. He has written *The Forked Flame: A Study of D. H. Lawrence* (1965) and *Dickens and the Art of Analogy* (1970). He argues in this extract that the captain presses his ship to such a dangerous extreme not because he is trying to help Leggatt but because it is a necessary test for becoming a complete captain.]

It is evident it is not out of a sense of obligation to Leggatt that the captain regards it as 'a matter of conscience' to take his ship so dangerously close to the shore, for he knows that Leggatt is a strong swimmer, and the mate has earlier told him that, in covering the distance of two miles between the *Sephora* and the captain's ship, he swam the 'last spell' of 'over a mile' without any rest. Nor does it seem adequate to say, as Albert J. Guerard does, that the captain is 'evidently compelled to take an extreme risk in payment for his experience', it not being clear to whom he owes such a debt. He would seem to be driven rather by a need to put both himself and his ship to an extreme test as a necessary preliminary to his taking effective possession of it as its captain. It is striking, in this respect, that the test should be depicted (as in the case of Leggatt's killing of the sailor) in terms of a holding on that is simultaneously a letting go: 'under any other circumstances', the captain reflects, he 'would not have held on a minute longer', but he does in fact hold on, letting the ship go closer and closer, giving it its head, as it were, until the 'black southern hill of Koh-ring' seems 'to hang right over the ship like a towering fragment of the everlasting night' and to be 'gliding irresistibly' towards it. The watch gaze 'in awed silence', but the captain lets the ship go on, ordering the crew not to 'check her way', until it seems as if the ship is 'in the very blackness' of the land, 'swallowed up as it were, gone too close to be recalled, gone from [the captain] altogether.'

Unlike Leggatt at the sailor's throat, however, the captain never loses his self-control, and at the last moment succeeds in bringing the ship round:

> Already the ship was drawing ahead. And I was alone with her. Nothing! No one in the world should stand now between us, throwing a shadow on the way of silent knowledge and mute affection, the perfect communion of a seaman with his first command.

Though the captain may start as 'a stranger to the ship', he comes to full knowledge of it as a result of this experience, the 'silent knowledge' that he has of it evoking, in its context of 'mute affection' and 'perfect communion', the sort of knowledge that a man may take of a woman. The captain, that is, sees himself as having fully taken possession of his ship; we see, furthermore, that he has ceased to be 'somewhat of a stranger' to himself, and that, having learnt to know his own resources, he has also taken full possession of himself.

During the manoeuvre, the self-possession he demonstrates in snatching the ship from disaster is shown to coexist with a capacity for letting go; just as his fitness for the responsibility of command (which he proves at the same time) is seen to coexist, given the way in which he risks the safety of his ship and the lives of his crew, with a pronounced tendency to irresponsibility. But the sort of knowledge he comes to as a result of the experience suggests the integration of these dark Dionysian qualities in a self that will henceforth be proof against their disruptive influence, for we are told that nothing can now 'throw a shadow' on his seamanship, on his 'perfect communion' with his 'first command'.

As the captain waits 'helplessly' to see whether the ship will come round, he reflects that what he needs is 'something easily seen, a piece of paper, which [he] could throw overboard and watch'; but he has nothing on him, and has no time 'to run down for it'. Suddenly he makes out 'a white object floating within a yard of the ship's side', and recognizes his 'own floppy hat', which he has earlier given Leggatt and realizes 'must have fallen off his head' ⟨. . .⟩ Conrad's provision of so fortuitous a saving mark 'to help out the ignorance' of the captain's strangeness is a weakness in the story, for it makes his achievement of knowledge too much a matter of chance—and turns the highest kind of seamanship into a tightrope of contingency. But the terms in which the hat is presented also suggest that it is not by chance alone that we are to see the captain as being saved. The hat which saves him is 'the expression' of his pity; and it is in more than a physical sense that he is saved by his pity, the 'sudden pity for mere flesh' that he feels for Leggatt from the moment he comes aboard, and which (among other things) makes it impossible for him to give Leggatt up to the captain of the *Sephora*. What his pity saves him from, indeed, is depicted at length in the story of Razumov in *Under Western Eyes*.

—H. M. Daleski, *Joseph Conrad: The Way of Dispossession* (New York: Holmes & Meier Publishers, 1977): pp. 182–83.

STEPHEN K. LAND ON THE UNDERLYING REASON WHY LEGGATT MUST LEAVE THE SHIP

[Stephen K. Land has been head of English and deputy headmaster at an independent boarding school in England and previously taught at the University of Virginia. He has written *From Signs to Propositions: the Concept of Form in Eighteenth-Century Semantic Theory*. Here he explains that the captain must get rid of Leggatt to maintain his own authority with his crew and the psychological strength his position requires.]

To give up Leggatt is the obvious and tempting thing to do and would correspond to the betrayals of the earlier political heroes ⟨in Conrad's stories⟩. Unlike them, however, the Captain at once recognizes as paramount the bond between himself and his dependent and has no thought of surrendering him to authority. None the less, it is not "right" for him simply to accept and identify with Leggatt, any more than it would be "right" for Razumov to join Haldin unreservedly, for Verloc to become an anarchist in earnest, or for Nostromo to give himself to popular insurrection. The hero's task is not to engage in the conflict, for both sides of which Conrad shows a roughly balanced mixture of contempt and respect, but to steer a way through it to a satisfactory and guiltless independence, such as is to some degree achieved by Emilia Gould and Natalia Haldin. The Captain, in particular, cannot accept as permanent and final his identification with Leggatt, for the obvious reason that to do so would be to condone indiscipline and to run the perpetual risk of the breakdown of his command.

The Captain must steer a middle way, asserting his individuality against both Archbold and his own crew. Here, as usual with Conrad, there are deep ambiguities on both sides. Archbold represents law and authority, the near-divine right of captains formerly expounded in the persons of Allistoun and MacWhirr, yet he is also shown to be a liar and an incompetent who fails to measure up to the higher standards of seamanship represented by Leggatt. The crew, while strongly inclined to be critical of their new Captain's unorthodox methods, are themselves given to indiscipline, particularly the first and second mates, who are both brought into line by the Captain as the story progresses.

To complete his course without compromise the Captain must avoid both extremes. He must neither surrender Leggatt to Archbold nor allow Leggatt to remain as a threat to his own authority. There are, therefore, two movements to the tale. In the first, the fugitive is taken on board by the Captain and successfully concealed from Archbold. In the second, the disruptive influence of Leggatt not only causes the Captain to act in a manner which brings him to ridicule and disrepute among the crew, but also has a psychological effect upon him adverse to the exercise of his new command.

> There are to a seaman certain words, gestures, that should in given conditions come as naturally, as instinctively as the winking of a menaced eye. A certain order should spring on to his lips without thinking; a certain sign should get itself made, so to speak, without reflection. But all unconscious alertness had abandoned me. I had to make an effort of will to recall myself back (from the cabin) to the conditions of the moment. I felt that I was appearing an irresolute commander to those people who were watching me more or less critically.

Having been brought aboard, therefore, Leggatt must be removed. The hero's own success requires that he not only save Leggatt from Archbold but also dismiss him, which he does in the second movement of the story.

This is accomplished when, with exaggerated risk, the Captain takes his ship at night dangerously close to land so that Leggatt may swim unnoticed to safety. The risk is psychologically and logically necessary, for the Captain, having accepted his responsibility for Leggatt in the first movement of the tale, must complete the second without renouncing or going back upon what he has done.

—Stephen K. Land, *Conrad and the Paradox of Plot* (London: Macmillan Press Ltd., 1984): pp. 170–71.

Barbara Johnson and Marjorie Garber on the Numerous Father-Figure Conflicts

[Barbara Johnson is a professor of French and comparative literature at Harvard University and a distinguished
literary critic and theorist. Among her many books are *The
Critical Difference* (1980) and *A World of Difference* (1987).
Marjorie Garber is a professor of English at Harvard University and the author of *Coming of Age in Shakespeare*
(1981). They examine here the many instances of rivalries
with father figures.]

When we turn to the second paradigm of psychoanalytic reading,
the pathology of the character, we discover a very similar Oedipal
conflict in Conrad's "The Secret Sharer." If by Oedipal we mean
competition with or rivalry with a father or father figure, or, by
extension, threatening figures who wield power and seem to disem-
power the protagonist, the story has more than enough such conflicts to offer. There are several candidates for the role of father,
notably the chief mate on the ship, an older man with "a terrible
growth of whisker," "round eyes and frightful whiskers," like many
emblems of castration in Freud (e.g., "The Head of the Medusa,"
"The Uncanny"), and, later, the skipper of the *Sephora*, also older,
also whiskered, a married man whose name might be Archbold (a
splendidly potent name) but the narrator isn't sure—he has repressed
it, and explains away the repression: "at this distance of years I hardly
am sure." . . . "Captain Archbold (if that was his name)."

At the inception of the story, before the arrival of either Leggatt
(the double) or "Archbold" (if that is his name, the nameless, almost
named, figure of fatherhood and the Law), it is the chief mate who
seems to threaten the narrator's authority. He is obsessed by
uncanny castration images—the mate's whiskers, the scorpion in the
inkwell—and beset by doubts. Do I have the right to be alone with
my ship? Is my command secure? Aren't the father figures around
me going to do me harm? As the story opens, the young captain has
decided on a demonstration of his own self-sufficient super-potency.
He will stay awake himself, rather than set an anchor watch, and
assume command of the sleeping ship. Feeling better, determined "in
those solitary hours of the night to get on terms with the ship of
which I knew nothing, manned by men of whom I knew very little

more," he relaxes enough to take heart from "the reasonable thought that the ship was like other ships, the men like other men." Heartened, he thinks of smoking a cigar ("Arriving at that comforting conclusion, I bethought myself of a cigar and went below to get it". Sometimes a cigar, when fetched from "below," from the unconscious, is more than a cigar. He stands confidently on the deck, barefoot, in his sleeping suit, "a glowing cigar in my teeth," the picture of male potency (or of infancy imitating male potency). At this point he notices something dangling from the side of the ship, something that shouldn't be there—the rope ladder. He realizes with annoyance that it is his fault the thing is hanging out—since he dismissed the watch—and that he'd better put it back in before anyone notices, since it is a sign of inefficient command. The excessive object thus doubles the cigar: the display of the phallus is both desirable and punishable. "I asked myself whether it was wise ever to interfere with the established routine of duties even from the kindest of motives. My action might have made me appear eccentric. Goodness only knew how that absurdly whiskered mate would 'account' for my conduct, and what the whole ship thought of the informality of their new captain. I was vexed with myself." Consumed with anxiety, with castration fears, he sees something in the water, and the cigar drops out of his mouth.

> I saw at once something elongated and pale floating very close to the ladder. Before I could form a guess a faint flash of phosphorescent light, which seemed to issue suddenly from the naked body of a man, flickered in the sleeping water with the elusive, silent play of summer lightning in a night sky. With a gasp I saw revealed to my stare a pair of feet, long legs, a broad livid back immersed right up to the neck in a greenish cadaverous glow. One hand, awash, clutched the bottom rung of the ladder. He was complete but for the head. A headless corpse! The cigar dropped out of my gaping mouth with a tiny plop and a short hiss.

The cigar drops out of his gaping mouth at the image of the headless corpse, the apparent realization of his castration fears. He is going to be punished by the whiskered mate and others for what he has done—or failed to do. But then the body's head appears, and, as in the Medusa story, he is released from his condition of stony paralysis: "it was enough for the horrid, frost-bound sensation which had gripped me about the chest to pass off." He is still intact—and so is the other. He is not guilty; indeed, it is the *other* man who is guilty, and guilty of murder, the murder of a "father" figure, the murder the narrator in part desires but won't and can't permit. Arriving at this point in the young captain's train of thought and complex of fears, Leggatt represents the part of the narrator he can't accept or integrate. The dilemma is posed; shall I integrate him? Shall I acknowledge him as part of myself? If I do, then I can perhaps have a sense of proportion about the guilt I thought was so unacknowledgable. I will not be totally innocent, but I will be able to take command without feeling so threatened by catastrophe. I will understand that the law is often absurd—that to take command is to be able to assume guilt and to issue arbitrary orders, to let the symptom go (open the portholes, sail too close to land).

The two versions of the murder story the narrator hears, one from Leggatt, the other from "Archbold," are both his fantasies. In one, Leggatt's story, the ship is in danger, the captain impotent and ineffectual, unable to give the order to reef the foresail, the other man is obstructive; he, Leggatt, acts heroically in the face of the fathers' failure, eliminates the obstruction, and saves the ship. In the other story, told by the skipper of the *Sephora*, it is the young chief mate, the rebellious son, who must be punished and disowned:

> "You see, he wasn't exactly the sort for the chief mate of a ship like the *Sephora*." I had become so connected in thoughts and impressions with the secret sharer of my cabin that I felt as if I, personally, were being given to understand that I, too, was not the sort that would have done for the chief mate of a ship like the *Sephora*.

Archbold would like to call Leggatt a suicide, to assume that he killed himself out of guilt. The "truth" of this primal scene is unrecoverable, and does not in fact exist; it exists only in its retellings, or rather in the narrator's retellings of those retellings, and both dramatize his unconscious fears, satisfy his unconscious needs: to be a hero; to be punished; to be a man; to be a child.

In the end, having harbored and released the fugitive, the young captain can be alone with the ship, with the command. He has come out the other end of the Oedipal crisis by accepting the necessity of losing a part of himself: his fantasy of guilty omnipotence. In essence he has arrived at a new, revisionary version of castration as *enabling*.

—Barbara Johnson and Marjorie Garber, "Secret Sharing: Reading Conrad Psychoanalytically," *College English* 49, no. 6 (October 1987): pp. 632–34.

[Cedric Watts is a professor of English at the University of
Sussex. The author of *Joseph Conrad: A Literary Life* (1989),
he also has written many other works on Conrad, as well as
books on Shakespeare and Thomas Hardy. He edited *Joseph
Conrad's Letters to R. B. Cunninghame Graham* (1969), as
well as many of Conrad's works. Here he comments on the
relationship between the captain and Leggatt and also illu-
minates the "structural elegance" of the work.]

Leggatt is described as 'the secret sharer of my cabin and my
thoughts, as though he were my second self'. This is a tale in the
Doppelgänger tradition of Poe's 'William Wilson' or Dostoyevsky's
'The Double': uncanny complicity, a symbiotic relationship, is established between two ostensibly contrasting characters. The captain
says that Leggatt 'was not a bit like me, really'; yet Leggatt also seems
'part of myself', 'my other self', 'my secret self' and 'my double'.
Conrad's enduring interest in kinship between a protagonist and an
outlaw gains here its most explicit presentation. Some of the reasons
for the bond between the hero and Leggatt are obvious enough:
both are young British 'gentlemen-officers' who have served on the
training-ship *Conway;* they are bound by caste and class. The bond
is also a matter of immediate, intuitive understanding. As is 'love at
first sight' in the realm of emotions (instant, strong, irrational), so
is their empathy in the realm of ethics. The stress on strange kinship has encouraged some critics to see Leggatt as some kind of
Freudian 'id' or Jungian 'anima', as a repressed part of the hero's
psyche, but this endeavour is resisted by the tale's predominant
realism, which establishes fully the external existence of Leggatt.
The tale does, however, adumbrate lightly (as a flickering glow of
suggestion around the strongly realistic narrative) a supernatural
covert plot, in which Leggatt seems a ghostly nocturnal visitant to
be encountered and exorcised. ⟨One⟩ passage, for instance, main-
tains the emphasis on Koh-ring (the island to which Leggatt
swims) as an Erebus, Erebus being the gloomy cavern by which,
according to classical mythology, the souls of the dead entered the
underworld of Hades. 'It would never do for me to come to life
again', Leggatt had remarked, provoking the comment: 'It was
something that a ghost might have said.'

The narrator says that Leggatt swims away 'to take his punishment'. At the realistic level, this remark is true only in the sense that Leggatt has chosen to begin a self-imposed exile as a fugitive. In the most obvious sense, however, the remark is a lie, since Leggatt is fleeing the punishment that would assuredly await him if he were put on trial for killing a man. Indeed, one of the most enigmatic features of the tale is that the narrator never seems to appreciate the moral enormity of his own readiness to help a felon to elude justice. Leggatt killed a man who impeded his endeavour to set a sail during a storm. He believes himself to be entirely justified in his homicidal action, since the sail saved the imperilled ship. The hero unquestioningly accepts Leggatt's view. An unsavoury moral implication is clearly that some men constitute a bold élite with the right to override long-established moral and legal principles. One elegant structural and ethical irony of the tale is that whereas Leggatt had thought it right to kill a man in order to save a ship and her crew, the hero thinks it right to imperil a ship and her crew in order to save a man. As Leggatt resembles a complementary mirror-image of the hero, so the eventual crisis on the young captain's vessel resembles a complementary mirror-image of the crisis on Leggatt's vessel.

The structural elegance of the tale is also illustrated by that detail of the 'white hat' in the sea. ⟨. . .⟩ The kindly gift has rewarded the giver, just as the captain's aid to Leggatt has resulted in a test of seamanship which enables the captain to gain confidence in his own authority over the ship. Like *The Shadow-Line*, this is a story of initiation by ordeal into maturity. Lucid, adroit, economical, elegant, 'The Secret Sharer' is both a vivid yarn and a tantalising rune. By depicting complicity with a violent outlaw as a near-mystical imperative with a valuably positive outcome, it displays in extreme form the defiantly Romantic and almost Nietzschian aspect of Conrad's paradoxical temperament. The tale complements *Under Western Eyes*, in which a fugitive is betrayed and the betrayer undergoes protracted anguish.

—Cedric Watts, *A Preface to Conrad* (London: Longman Group UK Ltd., 1993): pp. 134–35.

[Gail Fraser is an instructor in English at Douglas College in British Columbia. She has written *Interweaving Patterns in the Works of Joseph Conrad,* as well as several articles on Conrad. Here she explains that in order to become part of his ship the captain must accept Leggatt and his "other self."]

In 'The Secret Sharer', the plight of the outsider is more ambiguously treated. Part of the story's fascination is its reluctance to endorse in a straightforward way the young captain's decision to shelter Leggatt and help him evade 'the law of the land'. In this respect 'The Secret Sharer' dramatizes a familiar Conradian paradox, for the captain's immediate sympathy for the outlaw conflicts with his need to achieve solidarity with his officers and crew. His division of loyalties is represented as an intensely problematic division of self: 'I was not wholly alone with my command; for there was that stranger in my cabin. Or rather, I was not completely and wholly with her. Part of me was absent.' Conrad opposes the L-shaped cabin, which symbolizes the captain's 'secret partnership' with Leggatt, to the ship's deck and the 'established routine' of the community he ostensibly leads. In the story's dramatic ending, however, these contradictory stresses are resolved, and even before the Kohring crisis, the captain confesses that he is 'less torn in two' when he is with his 'double'. Earlier still, before Leggatt's mysterious arrival, he admits that he is both a stranger to the ship and a stranger to himself. To integrate himself into the ship's community as commander, the captain must first demonstrate solidarity with Leggatt, the outsider and his 'other self'.

In posing this dilemma of dual responsibility, Conrad adds an important dimension to the *Doppelgänger* tradition, which conventionally treats the protagonist's 'double' as a side of the self that has been hidden or repressed. 'The Secret Sharer' is like other fictions of this type because it explores Leggatt's role as counterpart of the captain's outward, public identity: to deny his existence (as in a lie to Captain Archbold) would amount to self-mutilation. In effect, though, it is the captain's moral feelings for Leggatt as another individual—a fellow officer—that set this story apart from works like Stevenson's *Dr Jekyll and Mr Hyde* or Dostoevsky's 'The Double'.

Conrad's allusions to the Cain and Abel story in Genesis, and his direct reference to the passage in which the Lord sets his mark upon Cain, gives the captain's act of fellowship a parabolic resonance. The contrasts between Leggatt and Cain are as important as the parallels. Unlike Cain, Leggatt kills an 'Abel' who is threatening the safety of the community; unlike Cain as well, Leggatt goes into the wilderness without 'the brand of the curse . . . to stay a slaying hand.' At the same time, the captain's instinct to protect Leggatt does not merely constitute an affirmative response to the question 'Am I my brother's keeper?' Rather, it involves his discovery of an authentic self—in the sense used by psychologists who give primary significance to the interdependence of public and private roles—by recognizing his responsibility for another human being.

—Gail Fraser, "The Short Fiction," in *The Cambridge Companion to Joseph Conrad,* ed. J. H. Stape (Cambridge: Cambridge University Press, 1996): pp. 40–41.

JOYCE CAROL OATES ON THE CAPTAIN'S PREJUDICE

[Joyce Carol Oates is the Roger S. Berlind Distinguished Professor in the Humanities at Princeton University. She is a Pulitzer-Prize nominee who has written numerous novels and collections of short stories, poetry, and plays. The captain bonds with Leggatt, Oates argues in this extract, because he is of his own class and background.]

The famous tale "The Secret Sharer," from Conrad's collection *'Twixt Land and Sea* (1912), similarly reflects the narrowness of its creator's perspective. Here it is class, not sex or race, that determines a man's worth: an immature young captain, uneasy in his responsibility, mysteriously protects a fugitive named Leggatt, who has fled another ship after having killed a man; the young captain goes to extraordinary, foolhardy risks to allow Leggatt to escape being brought back to England to be tried; by the end of the suspense story, with the flight of Leggatt, the equation between the two men, forged out of their similar backgrounds and temperaments, has been many times reiterated: Leggatt swims clear of the ship "as though he were my second self . . . a free man, a proud swimmer striking out for a new destiny."

The difficulty for contemporary readers of "The Secret Sharer," which was one of Conrad's favorites among his own stories, is that the bond immediately forged between the young captain and the young fugitive is class-ordained and narcissistic: Leggatt has even attended the captain's school, Conway ("You're a Conway boy?"). Leggatt's act of violence is portrayed as a virtuous act by an upstanding if hot-headed first mate; the man he has killed is of a lower social rank, one of the common sailors: "He wouldn't do his duty and wouldn't let anybody else do theirs. . . . You know well the sort of ill-conditioned snarling cur—" Why does the young captain so eagerly take Leggatt at his own word, and make no attempt to verify the story? ⟨. . .⟩ Where the Doppelgänger ("double") relationship between Marlow and Kurtz is mysterious, subtle and ever-shifting in its meanings, the relationship between the captain and Leggatt is superficial and far too heavily underscored. But "The Secret Sharer" remains one of Conrad's most characteristic stories, and it contains passages of language as beautifully evocative as the most celebrated passages in "Heart of Darkness." The opening is particularly effective, setting the tone for a tale of solitary risk and initiation:

> On my right hand there were lines of fishing stakes resembling a mysterious system of half-submerged bamboo fences, incomprehensible in its division of the domain of tropical fishes, and crazy of aspect as if abandoned forever by some nomad tribe . . . for there was no sign of human habitation as far as the eye could reach.

The silent approach of Leggatt, like a phantom in a dream:

> The side of the ship made an opaque belt of shadow on the darkling glassy shimmer of the sea. But I saw at once something elongated and pale floating very close to the ladder. Before I could form a guess a faint flash of phosphorescent light, which seemed to issue suddenly from the naked body of a man, flickered in the sleeping water with the elusive, silent play of summer lightning in a night sky. With a gasp I saw revealed to my stare a pair of feet, the long legs, a broad livid back immersed right up to the neck in a greenish cadaverous glow. One hand, awash, clutched the bottom rung of the ladder. He was complete except for the head. A headless corpse!

As if the young captain is the "head," the consciousness; and the romantic fugitive Leggatt the "body," the physical being and "secret sharer."

If Conrad's ideal in writing is to make us *see*, "The Secret Sharer," as brilliantly as "Heart of Darkness," frequently fulfills that ideal.

—Joyce Carol Oates, Introduction to *Heart of Darkness and The Secret Sharer* (New York: Signet Classic, 1997): pp. 11–13.

Plot Summary of
The Shadow-Line

Many critics see *The Shadow-Line* as the masterpiece of Joseph Conrad's late career. It opens with its narrator harkening back to the good old days of youth. We learn that he had been a mate on a good, strong, Scottish steamer that had an exemplary crew. Yet despite the fact that he had been most happy on board, he decided on the "rash" act of giving up his post. Apparently, blissful youth could not last.

> "The past eighteen months, so full of new and varied experience," he tells us, "appeared a dreary, prosaic waste of days. I felt—how shall I express it?—that there was no truth to be got out of them.
> "What truth? I should have been hard put to it to explain."

Yet, curiously, when the mate leaves the ship in the "tropical East," he waits for a homeward-bound mail boat not at the nearest hotel but at the Officers' Sailors' Home, seemingly unwilling to completely turn his back on the sea. It is here that we see an array of people that symbolize various paths that his life can take. He joins a table where the highly respected Captain Giles is rightfully sitting at its head. A man knowledgeable about both the sea and people, Giles relatively quickly and straightforwardly asks the young mate why he's given up his post. This antagonizes the narrator because he really doesn't himself know why.

Because of Giles's keen attention, the mate finds that the Marine superintendent of the Harbor Office, the gruff Captain Ellis, has asked for him twice. Ellis needs him to be the captain of a British sailing ship whose captain has died; the ship is headed out of Bangkok and on through the Archipelago. The mate signs papers and agrees to be ready by seven, now officially captain, "as if by enchantment." He is taken with "such a sense of the intensity of existence as I have never felt before or since."

The new master is full of joy at seeing his ship and first walking on deck. He goes below deck and sits in the captain's chair, thinking of all the others who had sat there and seeing his reflection in a nearby mirror. He is startled to realize his new chief mate, Mr. Burns, is in the room. Burns has an unusual long red moustache and is several years older than his new captain. He is unfriendly yet tells the narrator about his predecessor. The old captain, we learn, spent most of his time below deck loudly playing his violin and frequently would have the ship floating aimlessly. At one point, he had left his ship at anchor for the most part of three weeks, during which time he would make short visits to the ship while he had an affair with a poor yet strikingly attractive fortune teller on shore.

The crew had not seen him for a week, and when he finally returned he told Burns that he had decided to go to Hong Kong, a plan Burns knew was disastrous since the ship was unprepared for such a trip. After a few days on the dangerous course, Burns confronted the captain, told him they had to change course or all would die, that he was taking over, and that he saw that the captain was dreadfully ill. The dying captain cursed him and the crew, saying he wished that neither the ship nor its men would reach any port. The captain was buried at sea, and Burns brought the ship into port. There, he expected that he would be promoted to captain, but that was not the case.

The narrator finds nothing but delay in setting off. First the ship is held up while he must untwist a contract with a charter party that could pose trouble later. Next they are delayed because men on ship become ill. One positive result is that the captain is comforted by the doctor that comes on board, who points out that he has a respectable, good crew. The doctor also takes interest in the captain, just as the young man is beginning to realize what a lonely job he has.

Shortly, the steward contracts choleraic symptoms, is taken ashore, and dies in a week. Next, Burns is taken with a horrid fever. It is then that we first meet Ransome, the crew's cook. Ransome's first words are an apology to the captain that he won't be able to help much in taking care of Burns since he has to be forward in the galley most of the time for his cooking chores. He is intelligent and physically attractive, and is, according to Burns, the best seaman on the ship. He has signed up as a cook because of heart trouble that could make him drop dead at a moment's notice if exerted too far. He also offers to take on the work of the steward.

Mr. Burns is so sick that the doctor orders him to come ashore. The mate becomes panicked that if the captain leaves him he will die, and he asserts vehemently that his death will be on the captain's conscience. The captain decides not to leave him and puts them all at risk, since he won't have the help he needs once at sea. But more and more he feels that getting out to sea will be a refuge.

Once Burns is carried back on board, nearly lifeless on a stretcher, the crew prepares to set off. Yet once the ship is ready and unanchored, it is confronted with dead calm and unable to move. The captain goes below deck after wearying of the calm to check on Burns, who explains that they cannot move because the old captain has wished evil on them. The captain sighs, feeling even more alone. He not only does not have a strong chief mate, the one he does have speaks so absurdly.

Although the ship finally sets off, the continuing lack of almost any breeze allows only a slow, crawling pace. Regardless, the captain delights in the freedom of being on his own ship, finally at sea. Yet Ransome arrives on deck and calmly tells him that two men on board are sick with tropical fever, immediately destroying the notion that they will be safe at sea. Still, the captain believes that a true breeze "would have blown the infection away," and he takes comfort, at least, in knowing that they have plenty of quinine on board to help the sick men.

Ransome carries the doses off to the men, and the captain, rather than face going on deck, looks in on Burns and tells him about the other sick men. Burns himself is still very ill, yet determined to get well in the next few days to help the captain, who is momentarily comforted. Yet this, too, is fleeting, for Burns again speaks of the old captain, who is buried right along their course; Burns believes the old captain is trying to ambush the men and their ship. The new captain avoids Burns for the next few days and thinks to himself that since he received the command so easily that he is destined, perhaps, to have to pay for it in some way.

Indeed, not only does the air remain frightfully still, but more and more men become sick, until all have been stricken except for the captain and Ransome. Then yet another evil erupts: the captain finds that the remaining quinine bottles are filled with a useless powder. He is distraught, while Ransome remains calm. Burns, looking as if he will die within days, explains to the new captain his theory that the old captain took the quinine and sold it onshore for a good price. The new captain decides it is all his own fault, and the sickly Burns tries to convince him how foolish the thought is. When the commander gathers the men on deck and tells them the news and that the new plan is to try to get to the closest Singapore port, he expects it would be fair that they tear him apart, yet they stand by him. While he is in awe of their wondrous determination, at the same time he feels moments of near madness and even at one point hears himself talking like Burns.

There are not enough healthy men to keep watch, and the captain remains on deck for fourteen days with almost no break. Burns proves helpful in giving the captain good advice on their course, and Ransome attends to him and warns him about the darkening sky. A diary also serves as an outlet for the lone commander, who now holes himself in his cabin and writes: "I always suspected that I might be no good. And here is proof positive, I am shirking it, I am no good." Yet there is no escape; Ransome lets him know that the sky is getting darker; the captain realizes he must get back on deck, and there he confronts the blackness, the "closing in of a menace from all sides."

The few men left—"ghosts of themselves"—laboriously hoist up the main sail. In the dark, the captain stumbles upon a gasping Ransome; he realizes the cook has helped raise the sail. They wait then in complete blackness, and enormous raindrops start to fall. The helmsman loses his nerve in the whipping storm and the captain must encourage him, despite his own strain. Burns comes on deck, still dreadfully ill, as the wind goes still and then wickedly roars alive. He raves that it is the old captain and that he has been saving his strength to confront him. He bursts into mad laughter and then finally faints. Next the helmsman screams for help and must be relieved by another sick man. A new light is brought in by Ransome, the man "that noticed everything, attended to everything, shed comfort around him as he moved." With that, the weather clears.

A good, true breeze arrives, yet only two weak men are left who can work with the captain and Ransome to sail the boat. Then only the captain and Ransome are left. Forty hours later they make it into port, with, as the captain says, the spell broken by Burns's exorcising laugh, the wind in their favor, Burns wedged up against the helm to steer, and the captain and Ransome handling the rigging. As the sick men are brought off the boat, Ransome tells the captain he wants to be sent ashore and paid off. The captain is distressed but sees that the man is determined and fearful of his heart. He listens to Ransome walking away cautiously up the steps from the cabin. ❋

List of Characters in
The Shadow-Line

The *narrator* is young and at a crossroads in his career when the story opens. He has just taken the unusual step of quitting his job as a mate. He feels that he needs something more, although he has no idea what that something should be.

Captain Giles is an older, highly regarded ex-seaman who provides freelance navigational expertise. He prods, encourages, and advises the new captain and stands as an example of everything the new captain can become. He is mature, accepting, and keenly insightful.

Burns is the chief mate who wanted to become the new captain. Often he appears delirious, and it is unclear whether this is from his own fear of the supernatural, from his fever, or from some combination of the two.

Ransome is the cook who also takes over the responsibilites of the chief steward. He is a symbolic Christ figure, who indeed becomes the actual "ransom" by selflessly giving of himself for the sake of the ship and crew. ✾

Critical Views on
The Shadow-Line

[Joseph Conrad, in his introduction to this work, explains that the piece is not about the supernatural. "The world of the living contains enough marvels and mysteries as it is," he writes, and adds that his focus here is about the transformation from youth to maturity.]

This story, which I admit to be in its brevity a fairly complex piece of work, was not intended to touch on the supernatural. Yet more than one critic has been inclined to take it in that way, seeing in it an attempt on my part to give the fullest scope to my imagination by taking it beyond the confines of the world of living, suffering humanity. But as a matter of fact my imagination is not made of stuff so elastic as all that. I believe that if I attempted to put the strain of the Supernatural on it it would fail deplorably and exhibit an unlovely gap. But I could never have attempted such a thing, because all my moral and intellectual being is penetrated by an invincible conviction that whatever falls under the dominion of our senses must be in nature and, however exceptional, cannot differ in its essence from all the other effects of the visible and tangible world of which we are a self-conscious part. The world of the living contains enough marvels and mysteries as it is; marvels and mysteries acting upon our emotions and intelligence in ways so inexplicable that it would almost justify the conception of life as an enchanted state. No, I am too firm in my consciousness of the marvellous to be ever fascinated by the mere supernatural, which (take it any way you like) is but a manufactured article, the fabrication of minds insensitive to the intimate delicacies of our relation to the dead and to the living, in their countless multitudes; a desecration of our tenderest memories; an outrage on our dignity.

Whatever my native modesty may be it will never condescend so low as to seek help for my imagination within those vain imaginings common to all ages and that in themselves are enough to fill all lovers of mankind with unutterable sadness. As to the effect of a mental or moral shock on a common mind, it is quite a legitimate subject for study and description. Mr. Burns' moral being receives a severe shock in his relations with his late captain, and this in his diseased state turns into a mere superstitious fancy compounded of fear and animosity. This fact is one of the elements of the story, but there is nothing supernatural in it, nothing so to speak from beyond the confines of this world, which in all conscience holds enough mystery and terror in itself. ⟨...⟩

Primarily the aim of this piece of writing was the presentation of certain facts which certainly were associated with the change from youth, care-free and fervent, to the more self-conscious and more poignant period of maturer life. Nobody can doubt that before the supreme trial of a whole generation I had an acute consciousness of the minute and insignificant character of my own obscure experience. There could be no question here of any parallelism. That notion never entered my head. But there was a feeling of identity, though with an enormous difference of scale—as of one single drop measured against the bitter and stormy immensity of an ocean. And this was very natural too. For when we begin to meditate on the meaning of our own past it seems to fill all the world in its profundity and its magnitude.

—Joseph Conrad, *The Shadow-Line* (Garden City, N.Y.: Doubleday, Doran & Company, 1928): pp. vii–ix.

F. R. LEAVIS WARNS AGAINST OVERSIMPLIFYING CONRAD'S TALE

[F. R. Leavis (1895–1978), a highly influential critic, taught at Cambridge University and other colleges and universities in England. He was the founder and co-editor of *Scrutiny*, a quarterly literary journal, from 1932 to 1953. He wrote numerous books, among them *How to Teach Reading: A Primer for Ezra Pound* (1932) and *The Great Tradition: George Eliot, Henry James, and Joseph Conrad* (1960). This extract is taken from a lecture he gave to the Literary and Philosophical Society in England in 1957. In it, he outlines how many critics have missed the depth of the story.]

I won't push particular examination of the symbolism of *The Shadow-Line* further. You may say, if you like, that the outcome of the ordeal is the emergence of the young Captain confirmed and fortified in his vocation; proved fit and unflawed, the good seaman and Master Mariner, after exposure to the ultimate spiritual strains as well as the others. And that is part of the truth. You may take stock of the various ways, more and less subtle, in which he has gained in maturity, and finish with Captain Giles's concluding point:

> And there's another thing; a man should stand up to his bad luck, to his mistakes, to his conscience, and all that sort of thing. Why—what else would you have to fight against?

You may say that the moral is given in the final "There's no rest for me till she's out in the Indian Ocean and not much of it even then"—an adult acceptance of life as on the whole a matter of glamorless routine doggedly taken ("Yes, that's what it amounts to," Captain Giles confirms, as one Master Mariner to another). I won't dispute it. The point I have to make is that the significance of the kind of creative work ("dramatic poem," I have called it) we have in *The Shadow-Line* is such that it can't be represented by any moral. I have spoken of "symbolism": I have not meant to suggest that *The Shadow-Line* is symbolic in such a way as to admit of a neat and definitive interpretation.

It is a profound work, and complex in its profundity. Conrad himself (if he could be supposed capable of attempting it!) couldn't have provided an adequate summing up of its significance. If one perceives (as one surely must) that it is significant in the way of the greatest art, one knows that taking and pondering the significance must be a matter, first of sensitive response, then of a delicate balancing of one suggestion or intimation against another until the whole, in one's sense of it, has settled into the right inclusive poise. And it seems to me plain, that the significance of *The Shadow-Line* entails far more than the emergence from the ordeal of a young Captain who, sharing the same wisdom and maturity, can speak as Master Mariner to Master Mariner with Captain Giles.

Living back through the tale one has to testify that the intimation, the kind of resonance, the effect of transcendence, represented in the first place by the young Captain's reaction to the beauty of the ship plays a very important part in it. Let me just remind you of the effect made on the Captain (and on us) by the crew, so strangely at once so ordinary and so admirable: "The wastage of ill-health seemed to idealize the general character of the features, bringing out the unsuspected nobility of some, the strength of others. . . ." This kind of effect is developed in subtle ways through the ordeal. It is more potent in the atmosphere than the suggestion of evil associated with the old dead Captain. One remembers such things as this:

> The shadows swayed away from me without a word. Those men were ghosts of themselves, and their weight on a rope could be no more than the weight of a bunch of ghosts. Indeed, if ever a sail was hauled up by sheer spiritual strength it must have been that sail. . . .

⟨. . .⟩ And what I have aimed to do in sum is to send you to the whole marvellous work, *The Shadow-Line*. I have made no show of offering anything like a close interpretation or a full commentary. But perhaps I have said enough to suggest how completely *The Shadow-Line* disposes of the criticism that Conrad over-simplifies the human problem, is subject to "school-boy limitations," and takes little interest in the man who "tries to live by a gleam of inner truth rather than by accepted standards." For, I repeat, *The Shadow-Line* is central to Conrad's genius.

—F. R. Leavis, "Joseph Conrad," *The Sewanee Review* 66, no. 2 (April–June 1958): pp. 198–99, 200.

IAN WATT ON THE CAPTAIN'S RECOGNITION OF ISOLATION'S LIMITS

[Ian Watt has been a professor of English at Stanford University. He is the author of *The Rise of the Novel: Studies in Defoe, Richardson and Fielding* (1957) and the editor of *Jane Austen: A Collection of Critical Essays* (1963). In this essay, which some critics see as the best on *The Shadow-Line*, Watt explains how the captain grows to realize humanity's interdependence.]

The shadow-line is inward and social; approaching it one is only aware of some vague atmospheric change, and one may not know its cause; yet although it is mysterious and elusive, projected almost at random through the chance collisions of the individual with his endlessly varying environment, it has a compelling universality. The narrator, fleeing, as he puts it, from "the menace of emptiness," is really fleeing from the shades of the prison house that lie ahead; and he tries to alter his course because pursuing the present one—his career as first mate—obviously involves renouncing many other aspirations; it means acknowledging an end to the youthful dream that one will, one day, be able to achieve everything; it means, alas, beginning to be like everybody else. 〈. . .〉

At first, we observe, the narrator pays as little attention to Giles's gloomy prognostications as to the later warnings of the friendly doctor at Bangkok; unreasonably but understandably he clings to the belief that once out of harbour all will be well because the sea is "pure, safe and friendly." Such security, however, is more than anyone should count on; the crew's health actually gets worse as the lack of wind makes it impossible to pass the island of Koh-Ring; and the nadir is reached at the end of the fourth chapter when the narrator discovers that the remaining five quinine bottles actually contain a worthless white powder. He informs the crew of the catastrophe, fully expecting to be overwhelmed by their anger and reproach: actually, the "temper of their souls or the sympathy of their imagination" surprises him; and it is their stoic resignation, their refusal to see things personally, which does most to turn him away from his egocentric sense that all is merely a plot aimed against him personally—a plot by which he has been "decoyed into this awful, this death-haunted command."

Before then there had already been some signs of human interdependence, and of the narrator's growing awareness of it. In contrast to the moral intransigence he had showed towards the steward at the Officers' Home, he had listened to his sick first mate Burns's plea "You and I are sailors," and allowed him, sick as he was, to come back from hospital on to the ship, even though Burns, like Hamilton, had been his rival for the command, and was now so broken in body and mind that his mere presence on board ship was a serious hindrance. But when the crisis comes, Mr. Burns isn't wholly a dead loss: he steadies the narrator by telling him that it's "very foolish, sir" to feel guilty about the quinine; and he unwittingly seconds Giles's earlier advice about keeping to the east side of the Gulf of Siam.

It is, however, to the clear-sighted persistence of Ransome that the protagonist is most indebted. In the fifth chapter, after two weeks of being virtually becalmed, Ransome points out "a broad shadow on the horizon extinguishing the lower stars completely," and the narrator realises that there are not enough fit men to prepare the boat for the coming squall. Overwhelmed by the depth of his "contempt for that obscure weakness of my soul [under the] stress of adversity," he goes below in a state of paralysed remorse and confesses in his diary: "What appals me most of all is that I shrink from going on deck to face it . . . I always suspected I might be no good. . . ." Gradually, however, he becomes aware that Ransome is lingering "in the cabin as he had something to do there, but hesitated about doing it." Hesitates long enough to make the narrator ask "You think I ought to be on deck," to which Ransome replies "without any particular emphasis or accent: 'I do, sir.'"

It is the final nudge into the realisation that command means self-command. ⟨ . . .⟩

Here the vivid realization of complete human isolation in "the darkness before creation," evokes the historical dimension of the theme of human solidarity; the narrator, having been deprived, first through the loneliness of command, and then through darkness, of the support of his fellows, is brought face to face with the long tradition of civilisation since the creation, and his own utter dependence on it.

—Ian Watt, "Story and Idea in Conrad's *The Shadow-Line*," *Critical Quarterly* 2, no. 2 (Summer 1960): p. 133.

Gary Geddes on How the Captain Finds Meaning Through Work

[Gary Geddes is associate professor of English and writer-in-residence at Concordia University. He taught at various institutions across Canada and edited *20th-Century Poetry and Poetics* (1985), as well as other anthologies. He has published criticism, poetry, drama, and fiction. Here he describes Conrad's view that man uses work to help determine who to be and how to live.]

The question, How to be?, is central to the dilemma of the young hero in *The Shadow Line,* though it might be expressed as What to be? or To be or not to be? at different points in the narrative. Feeling the shades of the prisonhouse close around his late youth, he becomes disenchanted with his life and throws up his too secure job as mate. He drops out of the stream, not for political reasons, not in protest against any particular way of life, but in protest against the nature of life itself, its drabness, its sadness, its lack of interest and glamour. In the midst of his existential malaise, he views everything around him as part of 'the universal hollow conceit'; he perceives 'the sense of absurdity' that informs the affairs of men on earth; he suffers from a 'feeling of life-emptiness'; he considers his own life a 'dreary, prosaic waste of days.' The sudden disappearance of all mystery and excitement from the young man's life, producing what he calls 'this stale, unprofitable world of my discontent,' is accompanied by a vision of the world as a vast, inhuman machine. ⟨. . .⟩

The destructive element to which this Conradian hero submits is work itself, and the responsibilities and opportunities for failure or success that go with it. *The Shadow Line* follows on the heels of *Victory* and shares with that novel a preoccupation with the nature of involvement or commitment. Like Heyst, the young captain is a sensitive, inward-looking romantic; although both intellectually and temperamentally aloof from certain conditions of the physical world, he is nevertheless not satisfied to look on and make no sound, to remain a mere passenger in life, which is exactly what he will be if he books passage home. He contemplates the offer of a command somewhat hesitantly at first; then, as the idea throws him into gear and hooks itself firmly in the fabric of his ego, he jumps at it enthusiastically. The job promises not only to restore his 'feeling of wonder,' but also to help him in his search for meaning by giving 'opportunities to find out about oneself.' Echoes may be heard here coming from *Heart of Darkness,* where Marlow admits: 'No, I don't like work. I had rather laze about and think of all the fine things that can be done. I don't like work—no man does—but I like what is in the work,—the chance to find yourself.' So the vocational drop-out drops back in, naturally at a higher rank and in seemingly improved circumstances.

I do not mean to suggest that *The Shadow Line* is a treatise for departments of manpower; it is nothing of the sort. However,

Conrad does think of work as an alternative, if not an antidote, to paralysing despair and cynicism; he followed his own chosen vocation with relentless energy and insisted that his writing saved him from that 'madness which, after a certain point in life is reached, awaits those who refuse to master their sensations and bring into coherent form the mysteries of their lives'. Work, for Conrad, is something that stands between man and the vast indifference of things: it is, at least, a sustaining occupation; at best, it becomes a revealing pursuit.

—Gary Geddes, *Conrad's Later Novels* (Montreal: McGill-Queen's University Press, 1980): pp. 84–85, 87–88.

Stephen K. Land on Aspects of the Captain Embodied in Other Characters

[Stephen K. Land is the head of English and deputy headmaster at an independent boarding school in England and previously taught at the University of Virginia. He is the author of *From Signs to Propositions: the Concept of Form in Eighteenth-Century Semantic Theory* (1974). In this chapter on *The Shadow-Line* from his 1984 book *Conrad and the Paradox of Plot,* he theorizes that Mr. Burns symbolizes the side of the captain that confronts, whereas Ransome represents the side that succumbs to fear of activity.]

Both Ransome and Burns emblemize not only the weakness of the Captain's tendency towards detachment but also the strength which enables him, in the event, to overcome it. Burns, although bedridden, insists on being taken on the voyage and, once under way, becomes the chief exponent of the doctrine that the malice of the dead captain must be faced. "Skulking's no good, sir," he says to the Captain. "You can't slink past the old murderous ruffian. It isn't the way. You must go for him boldly—as I did. Boldness is what you want. Show him that you don't care for any of his damned tricks. Kick up a jolly old row." At the climactic moment Burns leaves his bed to come on deck and confront the spirit of his old enemy, which he does by laughing deliriously at the weather before he faints and has to be carried down again. His efforts are successful, as the Captain himself acknowledges: "By the exorcising virtue of Mr. Burns' awful laugh, the malicious spectre had been laid, the evil spell broken, the curse removed. We were now in the hands of a kind and energetic Providence. It was rushing us on. . . ."

The ship now has the wind she needs in order to make port, but to take advantage of this the Captain requires men to handle the sails. Beside himself and Ransome, all the men, including Burns, are too weak to do more than lend sporadic assistance in these operations. It is at this point that Ransome risks death from heart attack to save the ship. Ransome's heroism here reflects the innate professionalism and sense of duty in the Captain himself. Yet it comes into play only at the risk of death; and, indeed, Ransome does die in a sense, for the result of his experience on this voyage is that he decides he must give up his career as a seaman.

The name Ransome clearly implies a kind of sacrifice, and the man does risk his life and give up his work in the course of saving the ship. As in *Victory,* Conrad here uses a specifically Christian reference; the cook is called upon as if "to give his life a ransom for many" (Matthew 20:28). The implication for the central figure is clear. The inactivity which the Captain initially displays, like Heyst's detachment, is a sure path to personal safety if followed to the limit and without deviation. In a similar way Ransome's quiet and effortless mode of life as a cook keeps him safe from the threat of his weak heart. In action and participation, on the other hand, lie danger and possible death. Ransome's relinquishing of his secure detachment in order to resume the full responsibility of a seaman is a sacrifice which the story requires the Captain also to make. Ransome's sacrifice is emblematic of that which the Captain makes in coming to terms with his responsibilities.

Both Ransome and Burns represent the conflict in the Captain between detachment or inactivity and professional involvement, a conflict which has been decided by the end of the voyage with the crossing of the "shadow-line". Both men have therefore completed their tasks by the end of the story. Mr. Burns, who stands for the confronting and outfacing of the spirit of detachment, remains in possession of the deck. ⟨. . .⟩ Ransome, on the other hand, takes his departure. He represents the fear of activity which has now been overcome, and his removal from the ship, symbolically significant of the Captain's victory over his own psychological paralysis, occupies the closing paragraph of the story.

—Stephen K. Land, *Conrad and the Paradox of Plot* (London: MacMillan Press Ltd., 1984): pp. 216–17.

Jakob Lothe on the Power of the Narrative Structure

[Jakob Lothe is a professor of comparative literature at the University of Oslo. He is the editor of *Conrad in Scandinavia* (1995) and has written a number of articles on modern literature. In this extract from a chapter of his book, he describes the "far-reaching" implications of the narrator's very personal account.]

The prominence of the narrator is central to Conrad's narrative method in *The Shadow-Line*. The narration is consistently personal throughout: the protagonist relates a particular succession of experiences—revolving round a sea voyage during which he exercises his first command—that constitutes his crucial transition from youth to adulthood. The tale is the story of its narrator, at a particularly challenging and difficult point in life. And yet there are, as Ian Watt touches on when reflecting on the change of title from 'First Command' to 'Shadow-Line', far-reaching thematic implications attached to the subjective, introverted personal account. The most important implications obviously result from a complex combination of the various constituent elements of the narrative, and thus cannot be fully appreciated until the text is finished, or preferably reread. Even so, there are characteristics of the narrator's discourse that are more immediately observable. The most noticeable instance of these 'visible' narrative characteristics is probably the narrator's striking generalizations, one of which opens the story:

> Only the young have such moments. I don't mean the very young. No. The very young have, properly speaking, no moments. It is the privilege of early youth to live in advance of its days in all the beautiful continuity of hope which knows no pauses and no introspection.

One closes behind one the little gate of mere boyishness—and enters an enchanted garden . . . One knows well enough that all mankind has streamed that way. It is the charm of universal experience from which one expects an uncommon or personal sensation—a bit of one's own.

This beginning not only contains searching generalizations; it also tells us something important about their form and content. There are three points to be made here. First, the opening or prologue, constituted by the first four paragraphs, adumbrates a central thematic concern of the tale as a whole: a troubled experience of existence in time, and of life as a process not only towards adulthood but also towards death—a painfully self-conscious awareness of the aging process. There is a logical progression in the reflective generalizations. Early youth is idealized for its lack of temporal consciousness. Then follows one of the text's most striking metaphors: the transition from boyishness to youth is to enter 'an enchanted garden'. Simplifying somewhat, we could say that what the metaphor primarily signifies is the coming, the unstoppable approach, of temporal and existential consciousness. As the warning of its ending is 'a shadow-line', the novella's title, like the story background which follows, is eloquently incorporated into its thoughtful prologue.

Secondly, an interesting narrative characteristic is observable in the way these introductory reflections are presented. For they presuppose experience and hindsight; they presuppose, in fact, successful handling of the challenge facing the narrator in the main action of *The Shadow-Line*. One aspect of the generalizations here at the beginning of the story is that they are based, in a fairly straightforward manner, on the narrator's own experiences. This is, indeed, the main reason why they are so convincing—they are to a large extent verified by the incidents (and the narrator's response to them) later dramatized. This point bears some relation to a key one in this chapter: it is the distance—not only in time, but also in knowledge—which enables the narrator to focus his story on its essential aspects and to intensify the central experience.

Thirdly, the use of 'one' in the prologue should be noted. It certainly does not signal a change of narrative voice—throughout *The Shadow-Line* there is just one, that of personal narrator. Neither does the change from 'I' to 'one' suggest a radically new perspective.

Rather, it could be described as a subtle modulation of a stable narrative situation: a formalized (textually visible) invitation to the narratee to relate the insight suggested by the generalizations to those procured in his or her own life.

—Jakob Lothe, *Conrad's Narrative Method* (Oxford: Oxford University Press, 1989): pp. 118–20.

JEREMY HAWTHORN ON THE CAPTAIN'S EXCESSIVE SELF-BLAME

[Jeremy Hawthorn is Professor of Modern British Literature at the Norwegian University of Science and Technology in Norway. He has written *Joseph Conrad: Language and Fictional Self-Consciousness* (1979) and *Joseph Conrad: Narrative Technique and Ideological Commitment* (1992). In the following extract, he suggests that the captain's excessive guilt should be interpreted as a shocking recognition of his own limitations.]

Like many Conradian heroes, the young captain of *The Shadow-Line* is tormented by guilt—particularly about his failure to check the contents of the medicine chest at the start of the voyage. Some of the references to this guilt seem—to put it mildly—excessive.

> And I felt ashamed of having been passed over by the fever which had been preying on every man's strength but mine, in order that my remorse might be the more bitter, the feeling of unworthiness more poignant, and the sense of responsibility heavier to bear.

If, as T. S. Eliot has suggested, Hamlet's equivocation lacks a convincing 'objective correlative', so too does the captain's sense of guilt. He received a letter from the doctor letting him know that the medicine chest had been checked, and the deceitful substitution of the quinine by the previous captain could hardly have been predicted. Besides, the captain appears *not* to feel any guilt for a potentially graver dereliction of duty: his decision to take a sick man with him as mate when specifically warned against doing so by the doctor, thus putting the ship and the whole crew at risk.

An early reviewer of *The Shadow-Line*, Gerald Gould, argued that the work suggested a comparison with Coleridge's *The Ancient Mariner*, referring to the presence in both works of ships 'becalmed and bewitched'. There are passages in Conrad's tale which certainly call Coleridge's ghostly ship strongly to mind:

> With her anchor at the bow and clothed in canvas to her very trucks, my command seemed to stand as motionless as a model ship set on the gleams and shadows of polished marble. It was impossible to distinguish land from water in the enigmatical tranquillity of the immense forces of the world.

But more than such apparently striking visual parallels, what we can see as 'disproportionate guilt' also links both works. How do we explain this excessive self-deprecation?

The parallel with *The Ancient Mariner* and the importance of Christian motifs in both works suggest that perhaps we are dealing with symbolic portrayals of original sin, a concept that, by relating the condemnation of all mankind to the transgression of Adam and Eve, necessarily brings to mind the issue of disproportionate effects arising from causes unthinkingly initiated. And the Christian doctrine may itself be interpreted as a religious projection of human horror at the devastating results of apparently minor transgressions or omissions.

But a more psychological explanation is possible for the captain's excess of self-blame, and one which involves no supernatural element. His guilt is perhaps more a matter of shock at learning of his own limitations, or of the inescapable limitations of any human attempt to control human destiny, than a genuine recognition of extreme personal culpability. There is a highly ironic touch in the narrative at the point where the captain is waiting for the ship's first movement:

> 'Won't she answer the helm at all?' I said irritably to the man whose strong brown hands grasping the spokes of the wheel stood out lighted on the darkness; like a symbol of mankind's claim to the direction of its own fate.

Does mankind have a claim to direct its own fate? Or is this the Christian sin of pride, the curse of an Adam who believes God can be dispensed with? *The Shadow-Line* gives no unequivocal answer, but it does suggest that mankind must not rely on magic or benevolent gods, but must act as if we have the key to our own fate. The captain has good luck in getting his command; bad luck in what he experiences on his first voyage as captain; one cannot rule out the blind operation of fate. But he rises above bad luck by dedication and by habits of dogged endurance. Characters such as Hamilton, Burns, and the old captain are subdued and overcome by fate.

—Jeremy Hawthorn, Introduction to *The Shadow-Line* (Oxford: Oxford University Press, 1997): pp. xvii–xviii.

Plot Summary of
"Typhoon"

Convention dictates that if a short story begins with a description of a character, it should describe a major character, if not the main character. Yet "Typhoon" starts with a character's description that is so undazzling that one's expectations are immediately disturbed. Captain MacWhirr, we are told, has "no marked characteristics of firmness or stupidity." He is hardly the hero the reader is expecting. Additionally, it is quite curious that the traits that he does not have are explained first, rather than those that he does. As the long opening sentence draws to a close, the reader is told that he is "simply ordinary."

On the day that the story opens, the captain notices a drop in the barometer, indicating bad weather ahead. He is on board the steamship *Nan-Shan,* which had been sturdily built less than three years earlier for a firm of merchants from Siam. MacWhirr has been its captain from the start. He and his crew are traveling to the port of Fuchau on the coast of China, carrying cargo and two hundred Chinese coolies (unskilled laborers), who have amassed some cherished money and are on their way back to their villages.

The quiet captain, we find, writes long letters to his wife that relate great detail about each of his trips. She lives in a rented suburban home with their two children, who hardly know their father. Mrs. MacWhirr is pretentious "with a scraggy neck and a disdainful manner" and lives in secret fear that her husband, who signs each of his twelve yearly letters to her as "your loving husband," will some day come home for good. Letter writing by others on board also reveals more about their characters, how each communicates differently with his recipient, and how the men view their captain.

Soon after the captain realizes there is some "uncommonly dirty weather knocking about," the tension swells as we are told that while by law he had had to answer simple questions about storms in order to take charge of a ship, not only has he never experienced a furious sea, but he even forgets how he answered those few questions. As the weather intensifies, the captain starts reading about storms.

In what turns out to be the most the captain has ever said at one time, he explains to his first mate Jukes that he has decided they must go through the storm rather than waste time going around it as most of the books seem to be proudly advocating. He tells Jukes "that you don't find everything in books. All these rules for dodging breezes and circumventing the winds of heaven, Mr. Jukes, seem to me the maddest thing, when you come to look at it sensibly."

The story focuses not only on how man battles nature but on how man lives with, works with, and communicates with his fellow man. As the storm ferments, the young Jukes is relieved to be on board with his captain, yet, it is quickly pointed out, the captain has no such relief since he is ultimately in charge and therefore alone. When the two try to speak, only some words are heard, while the rest are lost in the gale. An enormous wave envelopes the deck, tossing and flinging Jukes so savagely that he believes he has gone overboard. Yet a sliver of reassurance returns as he thrashes through the onslaught and finds himself "somehow mixed up with a face, an oilskin coat, somebody's boots. He clawed ferociously all these things in turn, lost them, found them again, lost them once more, and finally was himself caught in the firm clasp of a pair of stout arms. He returned the embrace closely round a thick solid body. He had found his captain. . . . 'Is it you, sir? Is it you, sir?' he cried. And he heard in answer a voice, as if crying far away, as if screaming to him fretfully from a very great distance, the one word 'Yes!' . . . Jukes felt an arm thrown heavily over his shoulders; and to this overture he responded with great intelligence by catching hold of his captain round the waist." The narrator pokes fun at the power of intelligence here, for survival instincts are what make Jukes grasp his commander and what pull them through.

Aside from the chaos of the sea, there is chaos below deck, where the Chinamen have gotten into an awful fight, scrambling for their money that is rolling loose. The captain, who previously called them "cargo," insists that Jukes make his way down to break up the fight in any way he can.

When Jukes goes in, the captain also goes in, avoiding being "all alone" on deck. He goes to the wheelhouse, only to see men experiencing the chaos in greatly varying degrees: the second mate has mentally collapsed and rushes at the captain, who knocks him down. In contrast, the helmsman, who has not been relieved for hours and who has a face "still and sunken as in death" passionately exclaims that he can steer forever.

Back below deck, it is the boatswain, who Jukes doesn't like, who helps Jukes rally the deck men against the Chinamen. Here again, few words are spoken, but the men operate efficiently, the boatswain with his brute strength and the carpenter with his intelligence. The carpenter grabs some chain and rope and with the help of the other men subdues the coolies by rigging life lines around them. The seamen methodically collect all of the coolies' broken china, smashed wooden chests, clothes, and money and fling them into the bunker. Nearly at the moment that order is restored, the wind above board suddenly stops.

Upon meeting the captain on deck again, the youthful Jukes expects kudos for subduing the tumult of men. Instead, the captain warns that the books say that even after these six hours the worst of the storm is not over yet. But rather than experiencing the next rage of the irrational storm with Conrad's characters, the reader is told absolutely no details about it, only that the captain's wish that the ship not be lost came true: "He was spared that annoyance."

The ship docks in port and the men again write their letters. There is a longer section on Mrs. MacWhirr reading her husband's newest letter, alone. While the steward had been reading the letter surreptitiously with fascination while it was in process, Mrs. MacWhirr stifles a yawn when it's her turn to read about the horrific storm. Her only concern is that her husband not say he is thinking of coming home, since, after all, he earns such a good salary. Mr. Rout's letter, in contrast, reports little of the storm, says how clever the captain was, but not what about, and how much he misses his wife.

Mr. Jukes's letter "was really animated and very full." From his letter we learn how clever and fair the captain was to the Chinese. The captain and a few of the crew pick through and count the money from the Chinamen's belongings; they split it up evenly between all of the men, since most worked in the same place and for the same time. As for the few extra dollars left over, the captain personally carries it to the three that are the most hurt. Jukes explains how the solution made sense in numerous ways, but asks his reader what he thinks and ends with his comment on the captain: "I think that he got out of it very well for such a stupid man." One wonders how he defines "stupid." ❀

List of Characters in
"Typhoon"

Captain MacWhirr has none of the usual attributes of an early Conradian hero. He is a grocer's son, simple and factual, who speaks little. His excessive literal-mindedness makes him a caricature rather than a multi-dimensional character. His "bravery" in taking on the typhoon is shown as an overly logical response from a man who only exists in the present and who, lacking imagination and having never had a bad sea experience, has no reason to fear one.

Mr. Jukes is the young, somewhat inexperienced first mate to MacWhirr. He is smart, imaginative, and personable, and stands in striking contrast to his captain. He is a good man who undoubtedly will be a strong officer some day.

Solomon Rout, the chief engineer, is in charge of the engine room. His first name is fitting for his character, one of simple wisdom. He is seen as a friend by Jukes, is self-assured and the only man on board who knows himself and believes he knows his captain. It is ironic that he, the knowledgeable one, is taken by surprise by the captain's achievements with the coolies.

The *boatswain* is the overseer of the crew, whom MacWhirr likes for not being caught up in his position. He is fifty, immensely strong, hairy, and elemental, "resembling an elderly ape." The men like him also for his good-naturedness, except for Jukes, who sees him as lacking initiative and letting his men get away with too much.

Harry is the second engineer, quick with a curse and uncaring as to the violent complaining his captain might hear spew out of him. MacWhirr sees him as very violent, a man he has to get rid of. ✸

Critical Views on
"Typhoon"

PAUL L. WILEY ON HOW THE "HERMIT" CONFRONTS EVIL

[Paul L. Wiley has been a professor of English at the University of Wisconsin and is the author of *Novelist of Three Worlds: Ford Madox Ford* (1962). In this selection from his book on Conrad, he explains how man must redesign himself into a Captain MacWhirr if he expects to counter unknown evils.]

Bluntly stated, the theme of *Typhoon* is a version of Conrad's major topic of the limitation of human nature, or of the isolated individual when confronted by evil from outside his experience or beyond the protection of the community. Conrad develops the theme, however, by the dramatically successful interplay of two characters, Jukes and MacWhirr; and the clue to the story lies in an understanding not only of their relationship but also of the special function assigned to MacWhirr. Although associated as members of the seaman's craft, the two men are in everything else extreme opposites. 〈...〉

Whereas Jukes conforms, then, to the mean of human nature, MacWhirr is so exceptional in his unerring response to fact as to border on the impossible; and one can readily accept Conrad's statement that the Captain was never seen in the flesh. With his remarkable eye for defective door locks he represents an excess of the empirical as much as earlier characters, like Almayer, illustrate an extreme in visionary habit; and his complete dependence on what he can actually see, which is the mark of his originality, is accompanied by a lack of imagination great enough to isolate him from the commonplace world of people like his wife and Jukes. Although this very deficiency accounts for his dauntless temperament, it also leaves him tinged with absurdity; for his magnificent display of courage during the storm is wasted effort from the standpoint of common sense. His determination to take the ship through the storm rather than to deviate from her course is preposterous, based as it is upon contempt for the inherited wisdom of the craft of the sea contained in the book on storms. Yet the fault is not willful indifference to tradition, since in every other respect MacWhirr is faithful to the standards of his trade. The error results from a failure of the predictive faculty which is a safeguard to Jukes with his modicum of imagination. Without MacWhirr, Jukes could not have survived the hurricane and the ordeal of initiation that he undergoes, precisely because the test is utterly beyond normal human capacities for endurance.

MacWhirr's purpose in the story is clarified, therefore, when he is seen both as a measure of the limitations of the average man, Jukes, and as a warning of what is required of the individual who expects, as Kurtz expected, to survive evils outside the communal frontier. Only on condition, in other words, that man can equal MacWhirr by a radical transformation of his very nature dare he risk an encounter with the unknown and the powers of darkness. For a moment in the typhoon Jukes and MacWhirr are bound together, but their temporary alliance only emphasizes their separation in all normal circumstances. At the height of the story Conrad again calls, therefore, upon his device of dramatic allegory to strengthen the point of what must certainly be regarded as one of the great short masterpieces of irony in English literature.

—Paul L. Wiley, *Conrad's Measure of Man* (New York: Gordian Press, 1966): pp. 71, 72–73.

JOHN A. PALMER ON MAN'S REACTION TO
OVERWHELMING STRESS

[John A. Palmer (1926–1982) was a professor of English at Cornell University. He edited *Twentieth Century Interpretations of The Nigger of the "Narcissus"* (1969). In this extract from another of his books on Conrad, he reminds us that the author's focus in "Typhoon" is not on the weather but on how the ship's crew responds to the external chaos it causes, as well as the internal chaos caused by the Chinese laborers below deck.]

More needs to be said of "Typhoon," which has often been praised as a descriptive *tour de force,* and which helped create the reputation as a writer of sea yarns which irritated Conrad so intensely. "Typhoon" does have a rare pictorial charm; but its documentary qualities have distracted readers from the conflict of human motive and value Conrad set at the heart of the tale. As he insists in his Author's Note, the interest of "Typhoon" is "not the bad weather but the extraordinary complication brought into the ship's life at a moment of exceptional stress by the human element below her deck." And to see this "complication" clearly, it is useful to return momentarily to the closely analogous *Nigger of the 'Narcissus,'* a companion piece in more than setting.

In "Typhoon," as in the *Nigger*, the protagonist of the tale is confronted simultaneously by two forces which threaten to disrupt a rationally ordered situation—in the *Nigger*, the extraordinary gale which tips the *Narcissus* on her side and calls for the most heroic fidelity from her crew, coupled with the inner force of rebellion inspired by Wait and Donkin; in the case of "Typhoon," the impressive storm which jumbles normal routine and provides MacWhirr with a new standard of "dirty weather," coupled with the subcivilized rioting of the Chinese below deck. Conrad stresses the moral effect of the typhoon at the beginning of his famous description: "It seemed to explode all round the ship with an overpowering concussion and a rush of great waters. . . . In an instant the men lost touch of each other. This is the disintegrating power of a great wind: it isolates one from one's kind. An earthquake, a landslip, an avalanche, overtake a man incidentally, as it were—without passion. A furious gale attacks him like a personal enemy, tries to grasp his limbs, fastens upon his mind, seeks to rout his very spirit out of him." When Jukes's heart rebels against "the tyranny of training and command," and the crew begin to "grumble and complain," they are yielding naturally to the storm's power of shaking a moral frame of reference by threatening its metaphysical substructure.

And just as in the *Nigger*, a second threat is posed from below by a human element superficially exterior to the crew (Wait and Donkin are technically crewmen, but their refusal of duty sets them apart), and one capable of inspiring mutinous feelings in normally loyal breasts. Like Wait, the Chinese aboard MacWhirr's ship have the appearance of "bilious invalids" and introduce a principle of disorder associated with chaos and the lower regions (although Wait emerges finally to be housed guiltily above deck, the reader can hardly forget the powerfully symbolic scene in the chaotic carpenter's shop). The external and internal threats to the *Nan-Shan* are tied together through a disruption of order: the storm in its shattering of the *Nan-Shan*'s structure and routine, the coolies in their rejection of civilized judicial procedure. ⟨. . .⟩

"Typhoon" remains an essentially comic story, however, closer to "Youth" in mood and tone; and much of its irony is directed at MacWhirr. His approach to the typhoon—"'We must trust her to go through it and come out on the other side'"—has a simple strength, and Conrad's irony is mixed with affection for the Captain's dogged seamanship. There is even a hint of the romantic tone of the *Nigger*: questioning MacWhirr in the face of the storm, Jukes hears a "frail and resisting voice in his ear, the dwarf sound, unconquered in the giant tumult." But MacWhirr lacks the complexity of Conrad's major protagonists; his solution to the coolie problem—keep the whole matter quiet, and divide the contested money up equally—has all the sub-Solomonian wisdom of a too simple man. And the story as a whole lacks creative intensity; Conrad had merely remembered the ill-fated coolies, according to his own account, while "casting about for some subject which could be developed in a shorter form than the tales in the volume of 'Youth.'"

—John A. Palmer, *Joseph Conrad's Fiction* (Ithaca: Cornell University Press, 1968): pp. 80–82.

STEPHEN K. LAND ON MACWHIRR AS AN ANTITYPE TO *LORD JIM*'S JIM

[Stephen K. Land has been the head of English and deputy headmaster at an independent boarding school in England and previously taught at the University of Virginia. He is the author of *From Signs to Propositions: the Concept of Form in Eighteenth-Century Semantic Theory*. In this extract he relates that immediately after writing *Lord Jim*, Conrad wrote "Typhoon" and was experimenting with a new type of character. Whereas Jim of *Lord Jim* is the romantic hero destroyed, MacWhirr of "Typhoon" is the simplistic, factual survivor.]

Having completed *Lord Jim* in July 1900, Conrad began work on *Typhoon* in September and finished it in January the following year. *Typhoon* is at first sight an odd story for Conrad to have written at this stage in his work, partly because it has a comic ending and overtones, and partly because its hero, Captain MacWhirr, has none of the usual attributes; he embodies no paradox, is guilty of no compromise or desertion, and is pursued by no nemesis. The explanation seems to lie in the story's relation to *Lord Jim*. *Lord Jim* deals with an "imaginative" and "romantic" hero who is destroyed by an ultimately unbridgeable gulf between the realm of his aspirations and that of implacable facts. *Typhoon* is a study of a hero who thinks and operates on a purely factual level, and who thereby not only survives the kind of testing which Jim failed at sea but also proves himself a match for Jim in the field of colonial administration.

The story is more than a little tongue-in-cheek. The literal-minded MacWhirr is not a rounded character on the same level as Jim. His dogged and humourless conversation, pursued to the point of pedantry in his exchanges with Jukes, is caricature rather than portraiture, and his combination of utter simplicity with spectacular competence is generally unconvincing. *Typhoon* stands to *Lord Jim* in the relation of an exercise in thematic inversion, using, as it were, the major key instead of the minor and creating an effectually opposite mood. It is as if Conrad set out, fresh from the protracted study of Jim, to create his antitype, perhaps by way of experiment or formal exercise, simply to see how such a man might fare. That the creation was more a logical possibility than a psychological verisimilitude did not deflect him from a brilliant undertaking.

MacWhirr's situation about the *Nan-Shan* is very similar to Jim's aboard the *Patna*. Both ships are sailing in eastern waters under a foreign flag. Both heroes are surrounded by officers and men not themselves capable of confronting disaster. Both ships carry a large number of native passengers for whose welfare the white officers are responsible. And both vessels encounter accidents which make their survival seem, for a time, highly unlikely. The great difference between the two cases is, of course, that whereas the *Patna* is abandoned by her officers, including Jim, the *Nan-Shan,* under the captaincy of MacWhirr, is brought bravely through the crisis.

MacWhirr stays at his post and steams his ship through the storm because he is the antitype of Jim, a man of no imagination and therefore of no fear or impulse. He lives on a purely literal level, seeing only the most immediate implications of what goes on around him. "There were matters of duty, of course—directions, orders, and so on; but the past being to his mind done with, and the future not there yet, the more general actualities of the day required no comment—because facts can speak for themselves with over- whelming precision." Because he does not visualize the consequence of the storm MacWhirr steams into it without losing his nerve, whereas Jim, the visionary creator of the state of Patusan, abandons the *Patna* precisely because he foresees with graphic clarity the apparently inevitable results of her accident.

The relation between *Typhoon* and *Lord Jim* is cemented by the character of Jukes, who is first mate aboard the *Nan-Shan*, just as Jim was first mate of the *Patna*. Jukes, who in his own story contrasts with and counterbalances the figure of MacWhirr, is a paler version of Jim, a young, relatively inexperienced, but highly promising officer endowed with a hyperactive imagination. His inclination to inactivity as the ship is engulfed by the hurricane is closely similar to the detachment of Jim's last moments aboard the *Patna*.

—Stephen K. Land, *Conrad and the Paradox of Plot* (London: Macmillan Press Ltd., 1984): pp. 92–93.

JAKOB LOTHE ON CONRAD'S CREATIVE SHIFTING NARRATION

[Jakob Lothe is a professor of comparative literature at the University of Oslo. He has edited *Conrad in Scandinavia* (1995) and written numerous articles on modern literature. This extract is taken from a full chapter he devotes to "Typhoon" in his book *Conrad's Narrative Method* (1989). In it he delineates the shifting voice of the "Typhoon" nar- rator, its strengths, and the work's overall commentary on communication difficulties.]

In this final chapter, the description of Mrs. MacWhirr and her daughter ironically reaffirms and strengthens the contrast between two extremely different ways of life that has already been indicated earlier in the novella. Irony mingles with humour and resignation; the two parties are in every sense—not just geographically—miles apart. Underneath the humorous presentation of the failure to communicate, however, a more serious implication can be detected in this particular approach to what is a major problem in Conrad: his fiction contains few examples of genuine and mutually rewarding human communication. Considering these relatively rare instances, it does not take long to notice that they are often related to a sense of communication through shared work—not least in the well-defined and limited setting of a ship. It is important, therefore, that MacWhirr and Jukes, who embody very different personal characteristics, are helped, if not forced, to co-operate and communicate during such a major crisis as that of the typhoon.

Once the crisis is over, however, former positions are all too easily resumed—as Jukes's seems to be in the letter of his which effectively concludes the narrative of 'Typhoon'. The use of letters—both MacWhirr's and Jukes's—is an important variation in a narrative that at times appears somewhat monotonously authorial. Providing both information and personal views, Jukes's concluding letter reduces authorial focus on MacWhirr, but not without stressing his crucial role and impressive professional skills. The very last sentence again contains an example of curiously modified irony. There is an obvious authorial distance from Jukes here, for MacWhirr's performance during the storm clearly does not correspond with Jukes's adjective 'stupid'; and yet there is some truth in the characterization, as the simplicity of MacWhirr's 'face it' philosophy may appear to verge on stupidity. It seems just right that Jukes's letter concludes the novella; Conrad wisely refrained from adding an authorial comment to it.

Francis Hubbard argues that MacWhirr is fundamentally changed by his experience of the typhoon. If my interpretation of the novella suggests agreement with Hubbard's thesis, it has also—through the critical focus on the modulations of the text's authorial narrative, and the thematic effects of these modulations—shown in greater detail than Hubbard does how MacWhirr's change is indicated and dramatized. Although the narrative method of 'Typhoon' is distinctly less sophisticated than that of, say, 'Heart of Darkness', the various constituent aspects of this method—the authorial omniscience, the shifts of perspective, the use of letters, imagery, and personification—present several thematic concerns that are both persuasive and suggestive. In the narrative discourse of 'Typhoon', thematic simplicity promotes thematic suggestiveness: as the elemental drama of the *Nan-Shan* struggling with the typhoon accentuates human qualities such as courage, perseverance, and the ability to face up to loneliness, so it is precisely this lone, test-like fight on the part of MacWhirr that constitutes the basis for his change and makes him emerge as a wiser and more imaginative human being at the end of the novella.

—Jakob Lothe, *Conrad's Narrative Method* (Oxford: Clarendon Press, 1989): pp. 115–16.

Paul Kirschner Derides Critics for Their Simplistic Interpretations of "Typhoon"

[Paul Kirschner is a freelance writer and editor. He has taught literature at the University of London, the University of Geneva, and City University of New York, and has worked as an editor at the World Health Organization. He is a former vice-chairman of the UK Joseph Conrad Society and the author of *Conrad the Psychologist as Artist*, as well as many essays on Conrad. Kirschner also edited an edition of Conrad's *Under Western Eyes*. In this piece, he argues against the critics who see "Typhoon" as a relatively simplistic work. Instead, he congratulates Conrad for his ability to show the fragile and shifting balances between intelligence and instinct, imagination and intuition, and order and justice.]

MacWhirr, however, needs Jukes, who is even more 'ordinary' than himself, being 'as ready a man as any half-dozen young mates that may be caught by casting a net upon the waters'. He is as ordinary in his assumption of racial superiority as in his lack of talent for foreign languages, mangling 'the very pidgin English cruelly' when he speaks to the Chinamen. He may even be typical, at a time of England's greatest imperial expansion, in his faith in his own imagination, which here proves a handicap: ' . . . [he] had never doubted his ability to imagine the worst; but this was so much beyond his powers of fancy that it appeared incompatible with the existence of any ship whatever.' It is precisely because Jukes has these 'powers of fancy' that he is dismayed when they are exceeded. Yet MacWhirr himself is not as devoid of imagination as he has been painted. While Jukes's inmost feeling is that 'The men on board did not count, and the ship could not last', MacWhirr is shouting 'Rout . . . good man' and 'builders . . . good men'. Jukes can 'perfectly imagine' the appalling scene in the 'tween-deck, but only to characterize it as a 'disaster': MacWhirr thinks of others and even puts himself in their place, because in him imagination serves 'a humane intention and a vague sense of the fitness of things', rather than concern for personal survival or the need of self-affirmation.

Conrad nevertheless takes good care to dissociate Jukes from his homologue, 'Lord' Jim on the *Patna*. Jukes is 'daunted; not abjectly, but only so far as a decent man may, without becoming loathsome to himself.' For if he needs MacWhirr to steady him and tell him what needs doing, MacWhirr needs a ready, quick-thinking, self-respecting mate to remedy what is wrong, never mind how. The symbolic potential of the story is nowhere higher than when Jukes, giving way to despair, feels an arm thrown over his shoulders and responds 'with great intelligence by catching hold of his captain round the waist'—the evolutionary joke being that he is responding not with intelligence but by instinct. The ensuing image of the two men 'clasped thus in the blind night, bracing each other against the wind, cheek to cheek and lip to ear, in the manner of two hulks lashed stem to stern together' is like a brief symbolic vision of instinct and intelligence holding fast against a universe of manifest entropy. But the allegorical vision immediately dissolves into lifelike complexities of character and situation. ⟨. . .⟩

And so Jukes is last heard belittling MacWhirr while echoing his words. Jukes must believe in his own mental superiority to his captain, just as the engine-room crew must believe, for their own morale, that they are more important to the ship than those silly 'deck people'. In its delicate and complex 'equitable divisions'—between egocentric intelligence and species-instinct, imagination and intuition, order and justice—'Typhoon', far from being a simple story, is both the incarnation of a moral and philosophical vision and an artistic feat of the highest order.

—Paul Kirschner, Introduction to *Typhoon and Other Stories* (London: Penguin Books, 1992): pp. 9, 13.

[Gail Fraser is instructor in English at Douglas College, New Westminster, British Columbia. She has written several articles on Conrad as well as *Interweaving Patterns in the Works of Joseph Conrad* (1988). She describes in the following extract two of Conrad's stylistic innovations: his time in the story mimicking real time as closely as possible at a key point, and his ending that lacks a clear moral perspective.]

With 'Typhoon', written some two and a half years later, Conrad continued to break new ground. Although a 'storm-piece' like *The Nigger of the 'Narcissus'*, this story is concerned with the manifold ways in which the steamer's ordeal differs from that of a sailing ship. The division of crew members into 'sailors and firemen', the patently unromantic labours of such as Hackett and Beale, the increased isolation of the captain—Conrad portrays these historical changes in a manner that combines vivid particulars with symbolic heightening. As to fresh techniques or approaches, his own commentary is somewhat misleading: 'This is my first attempt at treating a subject jocularly so to speak' (*Letters*). It is certainly true that Captain MacWhirr's lack of imagination and stolidity of manner are portrayed comically, especially in his exchanges with Mr. Jukes, the ship's first mate. As we have seen in the episode of the Siamese flag, however, much of this humour rebounds on Jukes and carries a greater burden of criticism. Particularly in the matter of the coolies, Jukes's imagination and high emotions lead to an increasing lack of judgement, charity, and genuine insight. Of course this type of ironic reversal does not signal a new direction in Conrad's work. Rather, two of the chief stylistic innovations in this story involve the author's handling of chronology and the shift away from a stable moral perspective in the coda.

Perhaps the most celebrated ellipsis in modern short fiction occurs between chapters V and VI of 'Typhoon', when Conrad passes over the climactic fury of the storm with an understatement:

> Before the renewed wrath of winds swooped on his ship, Captain MacWhirr was moved to declare, in a tone of vexation, as it were: 'I wouldn't like to lost her'.
>
> He was spared that annoyance.

On a bright sunshiny day, with a breeze chasing her smoke far ahead, the *Nan-Shan* came into Fu-chau.

This leap forward in time goes well beyond Maupassant's dictum that fiction presents an '*illusion* of reality' through 'selectivity' and 'orchestrated events.' A post-modernist in this respect at least, Conrad draws attention to the art of 'yarning' (associated with Jukes) and challenges the reader's imagination to fill the gap. The impact of the ellipsis is all the greater because it follows immediately upon a very different type of narrative chronology. In his graphic presentation of the storm and its twenty-minute period of calm, Conrad makes the time of the story and the time of the narrative as equal as possible. The result is to immerse readers in the 'real' ordeal and to emphasize the importance of 'direct' experience as a source of integrity and wisdom.

'Typhoon' does not explore this theme without some degree of scepticism. In the coda, the story-teller's moral authority dissolves and we see the various failures of MacWhirr, Jukes, and Rout to communicate in writing what they have learned. In the central action of the story, however, MacWhirr's simple practicality and humane instincts take on mythic significance. The image of his single voice penetrating 'the enormous discord of noises, as if sent out from some remote spot of peace beyond the black wastes of the gale' suggests the persistence of these virtues in a twentieth-century context of 'alienation' and apocalyptic philosophy.

> —Gail Fraser, "The Short Fiction," *The Cambridge Companion to Joseph Conrad*, ed. J. H. Stape (Cambridge: Cambridge University Press, 1996): pp. 38–39.

FREDERICK R. KARL ON THE STRENGTH OF THE STORY

[Frederick R. Karl is a professor of English at New York University and has written extensively on Joseph Conrad. He is the author of *Joseph Conrad: The Three Lives* (a 1979

Pulitzer Prize finalist for biography) and a co-editor of *The Collected Letters of Joseph Conrad* (1983). In this extract, he enumerates the flaws in "Typhoon" and how it is redeemed by its storm descriptions and last twelve pages.]

Typhoon and Other Stories appeared the year after the *Youth* volume, but despite the various laudatory opinions of many readers, the four stories in this volume are not among Conrad's best either in form or content. Even the celebrated titular story becomes as dull as its hero, MacWhirr, whose sublime stupidity has often been generously translated by critics into a happy stolidity and heroic persistence. As possessor of many of the solid virtues, MacWhirr's personality simply cannot engage us; with his lack of imagination, his one-track mind, his ignorance of life, his blind sense of mission and orderliness, he is more a symbol than a person. MacWhirr's fidelity to duty surely bulked large in Conrad's view of a responsible universe, but the struggle of man versus nature in this story is an adventure pure and simple. Magnificent though the adventure may be, it loses stature by its very particularity. *Typhoon* is personal experience *per se,* without that forging of fact and fiction into an art form. Forgoing the story as a whole, we must finally return to the storm scene itself as one of the finest examples of sustained writing in sea literature.

Perhaps one of the difficulties with the story is its lack of surprise, either of word or structure. The form, as though following the central character, is simplicity itself—except for the last twelve pages which are a Browning-like presentation of various points of view as they bear on MacWhirr and his ship. In this rapid recapitulation which ends the story we have:

(1) *The revengeful second mate paid off and fired from the ship.*
(2) *Respectable Mrs. MacWhirr, far from the storm, living in boredom with her children and her daily emptiness.*
(3) *Mrs. Rout, wife of the chief engineer Solomon Rout.*
(4) *The mother of Solomon Rout.*
(5) *A friend of Jukes, the chief mate.*
(6) *Jukes' letter to his friend.*

These six short scenes provide an ironical contrast between the heroism on board the *Nan-Shan* and the complacency and placidity of life ashore. Furthermore, these scenes are presented through a sequence that is structurally sound—an attempt to suggest simultaneity of action and observation with a minimum of discourse.

—Frederick R. Karl, *A Reader's Guide to Joseph Conrad* (Syracuse: Syracuse University Press, 1997): pp. 144aa–144bb.

Works by
Joseph Conrad

Almayer's Folly: A Story of an Eastern River. 1895.

An Outcast of the Islands. 1896.

The Nigger of the "Narcissus": A Tale of the Forecastle. 1897.

Tales of Unrest. 1898.

Lord Jim. 1900.

The Inheritors: An Extravagant Story (with Ford Madox Ford). 1901.

Youth: A Narrative, and Two Other Stories. 1902.

Typhoon. 1902.

Typhoon and Other Stories. 1903.

Romance (with Ford Madox Ford). 1903.

Nostromo: A Tale of the Seaboard. 1904.

The Mirror of the Sea: Memories and Impressions. 1906.

The Secret Agent: A Simple Tale. 1907.

A Set of Six. 1908.

The Point of Honor: A Military Tale. 1908.

Under Western Eyes. 1911.

A Personal Record [Some Reminiscences]. 1912.

'Twixt Land and Sea: Tales. 1912.

Chance. 1913.

Works (Deep Sea Edition). 1914. 24 vols.

Victory: An Island Tale. 1915.

Wisdom and Beauty from Conrad. Ed. M. Harriet M. Capes. 1915.

Within the Tides: Tales. 1915.

The Shadow-Line: A Confession. 1917.

One Day More. 1917.

"Well Done!" 1918.

Tradition. 1919.

The Arrow of Gold: A Story Between Two Notes. 1919.

The Polish Question: A Note on the Joint Protectorate of the Western Powers and Russia. 1919.

The Shock of War. 1919.

Some Aspects of the Admirable Inquiry into the Loss of the Titanic. 1919.

To Poland in War-Time: A Journey into the East. 1919.

The Tale. 1919.

Prince Roman. 1920.

The Warrior's Soul. 1920.

The Rescue: A Romance of the Shallows. 1920.

Works (Sun-Dial Edition). 1920–25. 24 vols.

Notes on Life and Letters. 1921.

Notes on My Books. 1921.

The Secret Agent (drama). 1921.

The Black Mate. 1922.

The Rover. 1923.

Works (Uniform Edition). 1923–38. 22 vols.

The Nature of a Crime (with Ford Madox Ford). 1924.

Laughing Anne and One Day More: Two Plays. 1924.

Suspense: A Napoleonic Novel. 1925.

Tales of Hearsay. 1925.

Last Essays. Ed. Richard Curle. 1926.

Letters to His Wife. 1927.

Letters 1895–1924. Ed. Edward Garnett. 1928.

The Sisters. 1928.

Conrad to a Friend: 150 Selected Letters to Richard Curle. Ed. Richard Curle. 1928.

Lettres Françaises. Ed. Gerard Jean-Aubry. 1929.

The Book of Job: A Satirical Comedy by Bruno Winawer (translator). 1931.

Complete Short Stories. 1933.

Letters to Marguerite Poradowska 1890–1920. Ed. and tr. John Arthur Gee and Paul J. Sturm. 1940.

The Portable Conrad. Ed. Morton Dauwen Zabel. 1947.

Letters to William Blackwood and David S. Meldrum. Ed. William Blackburn. 1958.

Conrad's Polish Background: Letters to and from Polish Friends. Ed. Zdzislaw Najder. Tr. Halina Carroll. 1963.

Letters to R. B. Cunninghame Graham. Ed. C. T. Watts. 1969.

Congo Diary and Other Uncollected Pieces. Ed. Zdzislaw Najder. 1978.

Works. 1980.

Collected Letters. Eds. Frederick R. Karl and Laurence Davies. 1983– . 8 vols.

Works (Cambridge Edition). Ed. S. W. Reid et al. 1989– .

Interviews and Recollections. Ed. Martin Ray. 1990.

Complete Short Fiction. Ed. Samuel Hynes. 1991–92. 4 vols.

Works about
Joseph Conrad

Baines, Jocelyn. *Joseph Conrad: A Critical Biography*. London: Weidenfeld & Nicolson; New York: McGraw-Hill, 1960.

Barnett, Louise K. "'The Whole Circle of the Horizon': The Circumscribed Universe of 'The Secret Sharer.'" *Studies in the Humanities* 8, no. 2 (1981): pp. 5–9.

Batchelor, John. *The Life of Joseph Conrad: A Critical Biography*. Oxford: Blackwell, 1994.

Bennett, Carl D. *Joseph Conrad*. New York: Continuum, 1991.

Benson, Carl. "Conrad's Two Stories of Initiation." *PMLA* 69 (March 1954): pp. 46–56.

Berthoud, Jacques. *Joseph Conrad: The Major Phase*. Cambridge: Cambridge University Press, 1978.

Billy, Ted, ed. *Critical Essays on Joseph Conrad*. Boston: Hall, 1987.

Bloom, Harold, ed. *Marlow*. New York: Chelsea House, 1992.

Bock, Martin. "Conrad's Voyages of Disorientation: Crossing the Shadow-Line." *Conradiana* 17, no. 2 (1985): pp. 82–92.

Bode, Rita. "'They . . . Should Be Out of It': The Women of 'Heart of Darkness.'" *Conradiana* 26, no. 1 (1994): pp. 20–34.

Bradshaw, Graham. "Mythos, Ethos, and the Heart of Conrad's Darkness." *English Studies* 72, no. 2 (April 1991): pp. 166–68.

Brufee, Kenneth A. "The Lesser Nightmare: Marlow's 'Lie' in 'Heart of Darkness.'" *Modern Language Quarterly* 25, no. 4 (1964): pp. 322–29.

Burden, Robert. *Heart of Darkness*. Basingstoke: Macmillan, 1991.

Carabine, Keith, Owen Knowles, and Wieslaw Krajka, eds. *Contexts for Conrad*. Boulder, Colo.: East European Monographs, 1993.

Day, Robert A. "The Rebirth of Leggatt." *Literature and Psychology* 13 (Summer 1963): pp. 74–80.

Facknitz, Mark A. R. "Cryptic Allusions and the Moral of the Story: The Case of Joseph Conrad's "The Secret Sharer.'" *Journal of Narrative Technique* 17, no. 1 (1987): pp. 115–30.

Ford, Ford Madox. *Joseph Conrad: A Personal Remembrance.* Boston: Little, Brown, 1924.

Graver, Lawrence. "'Typhoon': A Profusion of Similes." *College English* 24 (October 1962): pp. 62–4.

Guetti, James. "'Heart of Darkness' and the Failure of the Imagination." *Sewanee Review* 73, no. 3 (1965): pp. 488–504.

Hamner, Robert D., ed. *Joseph Conrad: Third World Perspectives.* Washington, D. C.: Three Continents Press, 1990.

Hansford, James. "Closing, Enclosure and Passage in 'The Secret Sharer.'" *Conradian* 15 (1990): pp. 30–55.

Harkness, Bruce, ed. *Conrad's Heart of Darkness and the Critics.* Belmont, Calif.: Wadsworth, 1960.

Henricksen, Bruce. *Nomadic Voices: Conrad and the Subject of Narrative.* Urbana: University of Illinois Press, 1992.

Higdon, David Leon, et al. "Conrad bibliography: a continuing checklist." *Conradiana* (1968–) (originally published annually, now published every two years).

Howe, Irving. "Conrad: Order and Anarchy," parts 1 and 2. *Kenyon Review* 15 (Autumn 1953): pp. 505–21; 16 (Winter 1954): pp. 1–19.

Hubbard, Francis A. *Theories of Action in Conrad.* Ann Arbor: UMI Research Press, 1984.

Leavis, F. R. "Joseph Conrad." *Sewanee Review* 66, no. 2 (1958): pp. 179–200.

———. "Revaluations: Joseph Conrad," parts 1 and 2. *Scrutiny* 10, no. 1 (1941): pp. 22–50; 10, no. 2 (1941): pp. 157–81.

Leitner, Louis H. "Echo Structures: Conrad's 'The Secret Sharer.'" *Twentieth Century Literature* 5, no. 4 (1960): pp. 59–75.

London, Bette. *The Appropriated Voice: Narrative Authority in Conrad, Foster, and Woolf.* Ann Arbor: University of Michigan Press, 1990.

Martin, Sister M. "Conrad's 'Typhoon.'" *Explicator* 18 (June 1960): item 57.

McClure, John A. "Late Imperial Romance." *Raritan* 10 (1991): pp. 111–30.

McLauchlan, Juliet. "The 'Value' and 'Significance' of 'Heart of Darkness.'" *Conradiana* 15 (1983): pp. 3–21.

Murfin, Ross C., ed. *Joseph Conrad: Heart of Darkness.* Boston: St. Martin's, 1996.

Najder, Zdzislaw. *Joseph Conrad: A Chronicle.* Tr. Halina Carroll-Najder. New Brunswick, N.J.: Rutgers University Press; Cambridge: Cambridge University Press, 1983.

Navarette, Susan J. "The Anatomy of Failure in Joseph Conrad's 'Heart of Darkness.'" *Texas Studies in Literature and Language* 35 (1993): pp. 279–315.

Paccaud, Josiane. "Under the Other's Eyes: Conrad's 'The Secret Sharer.'" *Conradian* 12 (1987): pp. 59–73.

Purdy, Dwight H. "Conrad at Work: The Two Serial Texts of 'Typhoon.'" *Conradiana* 19 (1987): pp. 99–119.

Reid, Stephen A. "The 'Unspeakable Rites' in *Heart of Darkness.*" *Modern Fiction Studies* 9, no. 4 (1963–64): pp. 347–56.

Ressler, Steve. "Conrad's 'The Secret Sharer': Affirmation of Action." *Conradiana* 16, no. 3 (1984): pp. 195–214.

Rising, Catharine. *Darkness at Heart: Fathers and Sons in Conrad.* Westport, Conn.: Greenwood Press, 1990.

Schuster, Charles I. "Comedy and the Limits of Language in Conrad's 'Typhoon.'" *Conradiana* 16 (1984): pp. 55–71.

Shaffer, Brian W. "'Rebarbarizing Civilization': Conrad's African Fiction and Spencerian Sociology." *PMLA* 108 (1993): pp. 45–58.

Sherry, Norman. *Conrad and His World.* London: Thames & Hudson, 1972.

Stallman, Robert W. "Conrad and 'The Secret Sharer.'" *Accent* 9 (Spring 1949): pp. 131–43.

Straus, Nina Pelikan. "The Exclusion of the Intended from Secret Sharing in Conrad's 'Heart of Darkness.'" *Novel* 20, no. 2 (1987): pp. 123–37.

Watt, Ian. *Conrad in the Nineteenth Century.* Berkeley: University of California Press, 1979.

Watts, Cedric. "'A Bloody Racist': About Achebe's View of Conrad." *Yearbook of English Studies* 13 (1983): pp. 196–209.

———. *Joseph Conrad: A Literary Life*. London: Macmillan, 1989.

Wegelin, Christof. "MacWhirr and the Testimony of the Human Voice." *Conradiana* 7 (1975): pp. 45–50.

Wills, John H. "Conrad's 'Typhoon': A Triumph of Organic Art." *North Dakota Quarterly* 30 (1962): pp. 62–70.

Zabel, Morton Dauwen. "Conrad: The Secret Sharer." *New Republic* 104, no. 16 (21 April 1941): pp. 567–74.

Index of
Themes and Ideas